Your First Year of Homeschooling

A CHRISTIAN MOM'S GUIDE TO BALANCING FAITH, FAMILY, AND YOUR CHILD'S EDUCATION

(WHILE TAKING CARE OF YOURSELF)

ELIZABETH JENKINS

Your First Year of Homeschooling

A Christian Mom's Guide to Balancing Faith,
Family, and Your Child's Education
(While Taking Care of Yourself)

by
Elizabeth Jenkins

Published by

Christian Book Council

Copyright © 2010 - All rights reserved.

Contact info:

KRE Book Group
PO Box 121135
Nashville, TN 37212

For more information on
this series, please visit us
on the web at

ChristianBookCouncil.com

Table of Contents
ℰꝲ ℭℛ

DEDICATION

Thank you to my wonderful husband Timothy as well as my beautiful children Ashley and Charlie.

Thank you to all the homeschooling moms who shared their experiences with me as I wrote this book.

Also, thank you to all of those brave women who choose to homeschool their children. You are all an inspiration to me.

Thank you, God, for bringing me such amazing blessings every day.

CHAPTER ONE

FINDING ENJOYMENT IN HOMESCHOOLING

(FOR BOTH YOU AND YOUR KIDS)

Homeschooling is an adventure to be sure – a journey through the unknown wilderness of the 21st century. Lewis and Clark may have had to deal with savage natives, wild and angry bears, and thousands of miles of treacherous terrain 250-plus years ago, but you, dear homeschooling mother, have to learn how to navigate dirty dishes, grumpy and uncooperative students, unsupportive friends and family member,; a spouse who wants and needs more attention than you have the energy to give, and sometimes you even have to throw in a part-

(or – gasp!) full-time job. Whew! Makes the wilderness look pretty tempting, doesn't it?

Want to save your sanity and actually enjoy the experience of teaching your kids at home? Then you are going to have to learn a few lessons yourself.

Lesson #1:

Stop trying to create the perfect homeschool environment.

It's time to let go of whatever romanticized notion of homeschooling you are trying to live up to. What do I mean by that? Let's look at two scenarios: the one we *think* that homeschooling should be and the one it *really* is:

Scenario No. 1:

Here's the homeschool we all wish we had; you know, the homeschool that looks like this: perfectly behaved children sitting around the kitchen table while a calm, gentle, soft-spoken mother explains how rockets launch into the air. Everyone is engrossed in her explanation, anxious to learn more. They finish their science lesson and move onto math with no complaining and eager anticipation. Meanwhile the dishwasher hums softly; the washing machine drones in a far-off area of the house and dinner slowly cooks in a crockpot on the counter, filling the house with an inviting aroma. The day continues in a relaxed and joyful atmosphere.

Scenario No. 2:

Now, let's look at a real homeschool: A frazzled mother who has barely had time to brush her teeth sneaks a bite of a donut as her children scatter in hopes of not having to move on to math. Her 5-year-old yells from upstairs that the toilet is blocked. The mother scurries up the stairs with plunger in hand, tripping over heaps of dirty laundry waiting in the hallway to make their way to the laundry room. Meanwhile her 10-year-old is complaining that he can't find his math book and her 13-year-old daughter is yelling that she can't concentrate when everyone is being so noisy. The dog jumps up on the counter and snatches leftover waffles from someone's dirty plate. And it's only 9:15 a.m.!

Does your homeschool sound more like scenario No. 2? Take heart, you are not alone. I began my own homeschool journey with a lot of expectations and a lot of plans. As a Christian parent whose children had been attending a traditional Christian school since kindergarten, I wanted (no, *needed*), to add the same spiritual depth to our school day. I did not want to just teach history and English and science. I wanted to teach my children the important part God plays in everything. So I began looking for just the right mix of academic and Christian-based curriculum. With so many choices, it was difficult to sort through the variety to find just the right mix for us. It wasn't long before I realized that taking a more spiritual route of education wasn't going to be easy. Just because our homeschool was going to focus on God's role in our lives didn't mean that my children would be perfectly focused and diligent in all things; oftentimes the exact opposite happened.

I had talked to several Christian families who homeschooled and their days seemed so harmonious and loving and compassionate (from the outside, at least), and I expected the same in our classroom. It wasn't until later that I discovered that every homeschooling family must deal with the same discipline, focus and attention issues; –whether Christian or not.

In addition to dealing with my own expectations regarding my children's spiritual strengths and weaknesses, I also had to deal with coming to grips with the daily grind of the academic aspect of homeschooling.

Positive that I had thought of everything, I began week one with detailed lesson schedules and a tough-as-nails attitude. By week 10 we had already ditched our spelling curriculum, had changed our daily and weekly schedules four times, and were beginning to rethink our entire approach to learning. My house was a mess. I was about two weeks behind with my own writing assignments and one day when we went to make lunch we realized that no one had been to the grocery store for real food since the first month of school. Arghh! Homeschooling had indeed gotten the best of me and we weren't even through the first semester yet!

Lesson #2:

Be brutally honest.

How did I survive? First, by getting honest. If we're all honest, most of us will admit that more of our homeschool days resemble chaos than calm, and that's OK. To prove that fact (and feel better about my own situation), I recently spent a day in a local elementary classroom and realized that their day looked a lot like ours, only on a larger, more chaotic scale. One child forgot his book, another kept staring out a window, a third threw up all over his desk (and worksheets), two more in the corner continued to bicker throughout the morning, and the teacher looked tired ... oh, so very tired.

Life is hectic whether you work at home full time or in a classroom all day. The key to finding a way to not just survive, but thrive, is to find the freedom to create the learning environment that works best for your individual family and circumstances.

Remember, just because you are focusing your homeschool efforts on building your children's character as well as building their reading and other academic skills does not mean it will be easy – or every day will yield success. Be prepared for setbacks and admit when you have set your goals too high. Trying to make your children live up to some preconceived notions of academic and spiritual success will only breed discontent and frustration. Instead, be honest about your limits (and theirs) and work around everyone's abilities. There will be plenty of time to tackle those hard-to-get concepts. Thankfully, homeschooling gives you and your children the time to work on harder subjects and skills at your own pace.

Lesson #3:

Ditch the guilt.

The next step on the journey toward creating a true homeschool haven is to get rid of the guilt! Stop struggling to juggle it all: housework, kids; school, church, an outside job. Give yourself permission to get tired and make mistakes. Everyone does. Even those professional teachers at "real school" get overwhelmed, frustrated and burned out, so why shouldn't you?

Let the house run amuck for a day or two. Eat off of paper plates if you have to. Let the kids "forget" to do their math lesson today. Instead, cuddle up together with a good book or go outside and play in the rain – and the mud! Enjoy the moment. Homeschooling doesn't have to be one hassle after another. It can – and should – be fun for all of you! The key is learning to survive not just minute by minute, day by day, month by month and year by year, but by enjoying what you can and letting the rest go.

Lesson #4:

Take time for yourself.

There's a lot on your plate right, but that should not mean that you do not take time out to relax and rejuvenate. For some mothers that may mean working out every morning, while others just want five minutes to sip a leisurely cup of tea. Maybe you need to get away once a month all by yourself (or with your spouse), or maybe taking time to meet your own needs means just taking a walk *alone* every evening. For many moms, taking just a few minutes each morning in concentrated prayer, asking for patience, diligence and guidance throughout the rest of the day, is all that is needed to begin the morning on the right path – and stay on it throughout the day, no matter how hectic it becomes.

Taking time out doesn't have to be consuming or even expensive. It actually can be quite simple. The hardest part is admitting that you deserve it!

Lesson #5:

Let the spiritual element of your homeschool help calm your days, not create more chaos.

When Christian parents decide to home-school, they often end up adding even more chores and frustration to their day. Trying to add in a time for devotion and prayer as well as a Bible lesson and discussion can be too much to handle, especially if you are trying to work individually with children. Adding a spiritual element to your homeschool should help calm your day, not create more chaos. Maybe you can't find time for a corporate prayer. That's OK. Instead of studying specific Bible passages, take some time while studying current events to pray for the people you read about in the newspaper. When studying a certain part of the world, see if your church has a missionary there and write them a letter. Or simply talk about the wonders of God's creation when studying science instead of doing an in-depth unit of the falsehoods of evolution. The most important thing when devising a Christian education plan is figuring out what you think is important for your children to learn and finding subtle ways to incorporate those teachings into your overall curriculum – not necessary to add subjects and topics to your daily class work.

These are just a few of the many lessons to be covered within the following pages. Whether you are a seasoned homeschool administrator who needs help to get organized, get more done, and save your sanity, or a brand new homeschooling parent who is feeling overwhelmed by the demands you are putting on yourself and your kids to keep up with "schooled kids," than this book is for you!

Not the average homeschooling manual, this book is less of a "how-to-homeschool" guide and more of a "how-to-create,-regain-and-rebalance-you-life" tip book. Going beyond the typical generalities of organizing a typical school day and choosing the right curriculum, this book offers insight and wisdom into the concerns every homeschooling parent faces, but often does not want to admit, including:

- Feeling Overwhelmed (or even like a complete failure)

- Dealing with Bad Days

- Handling the Objections (and sometimes rude advice) of Others

- Taking a Time Out for Yourself

- Figuring Out How to Fit It All Into a 24-hour Day

- Keeping Your Spousal Relationship Alive

- And More ...

Homeschooling can be a real challenge, especially if you do not face the struggles with honestly and understanding. The good news is that success is yours. All you have to do is ... Oh, did I say I had all the answers? Keep reading and find out!

CHAPTER TWO

YOUR CHOICE TO HOMESCHOOL: LETTING GO OF THE GUILT

(AND SHUTTING UP THOSE NAYSAYERS)

Nothing saps your energy or your time more than fighting your own guilt – and others expectations.

If anyone tells you that they have this homeschooling journey figured out they are either:

1. living in a dream world; or

2. lying

The fact is we are all struggling to figure out our place in this homeschooling journey we find ourselves in. I've talked to mothers who have been homeschooling 20 years, and those who have been homeschooling for two months and eventually they all voice the same guilty concerns: The house is a wreck; their husband complains he does not get enough spousal attention (and he probably doesn't) and each kid claims that they are being left in the dust (you work with him more ... you love her the best ...) and so on.

If you are left at the end of the day wondering if you did it right – if you did anything right – take heart. Every one of us feels the same way at least 100 times each week. Motherhood is an all-encompassing, overwhelming job. Throw in the responsibility of educating your children and preparing them to take their place in the world and your days may seem like an endless stream of overwhelming tasks that leave you wondering if what you are doing is good enough.

Ditch the guilt. Homeschooling is an ever-changing medium, which means that there will be good days and there will be bad days. There will be weeks when you and your children accomplish a lot; and there will be weeks when it seems that you have been stuck on fractions for a lifetime (and maybe you have).

But here's the good news: if your children were in "regular" school they would have good days and bad days, productive weeks and unproductive weeks. The odds are that each of your children would also come across a few teachers that would not be able to teach them a thing. Aren't those wasted years? And there would be times when your child would struggle; only instead of taking their time until they "get it," the class would move forward at breakneck speed leaving your child in the dust.

Angela told me an interesting story a few months ago that has stuck in my head. Her daughter had been having a horrible time in math in sixth grade. By February, they had only been able to master about one-third of the textbook for the year. Desperate for help, Angela met with the math teacher at the local middle school, hoping for some guidance. The teacher, a wonderful man who just happened to be a homeschool advocate (you don't find that often in public school officials), explained to Angela that had her daughter been in his class she would be almost through the book. But, he stressed, she wouldn't understand a thing. "I would have had to move on each time she struggled. Left not understanding the first step, she would have been lost by week four or five and would have never caught up. She would have failed. I see this all of the time," he continued. "Some kids just need more time and more practice. I can't give them what they need and if their parents don't help them or find them a tutor they are left lost and frustrated. It's a shame really. So, your daughter only finished half the book this year and picks up where she left off in seventh grade. Isn't it better that she actually learns the stuff rather than pushing through just to finish a book?" Now that's a story that every homeschool mom should remember!

Here is another tidbit from a good friend that has been homeschooling for almost 23 years. As I struggled to decide if I could actually homeschool my kids, Sarah asked why I was so worried. I explained that I worried that I would really mess up my kids' education. After all, there education is the basis for their success in life. She nodded her head and looked at me. "Didn't you say you were going to take this one year at a time? That you would reevaluate every spring and decide whether or not to send them back to school each fall or keep them home another year?"

"Yes," I said.

"Then what's the problem?" she asked. "Do you honestly think you can mess up your kids so badly that it completely ruins their academic career in only nine months? Unless you do absolutely nothing with them all year, they're bound to learn something – despite your best efforts to the contrary!"

I have clung to that guilt-freeing statement ever since. On those days when I am positive that my children will be morons because of my lack of discipline or knowledge, I remember: I can't screw them up that badly in just a few months. And guess what? In our first year of homeschooling both of my children tested three grade levels ahead in almost every subject. Guess the guilt really was fruitless after all!

Now, what about all of those naysayers? Are they playing on your guilt too? Forget them. I know, I know, that's easier said than done, especially when well-meaning folks call you on the phone to ask how school is going, only to go into a narrative about how unsocialized children can't hack the real world or how Johnny down the street just won the national spelling bee because of the wonderful job the public school is doing (what about the thousands of other kids in the school who can't even read at grade level?).

The fact is that sometimes it can be easier to deal with strangers on the street who question your ability to homeschool than those closest to you. In my case, it was my mother. Every week I would speak to her on the phone to give her an update on the family. Inevitably she would ask how school was going. I would continue to tell her about all the great subjects we were covering; how my daughter was very involved in local community theater and how my son had just earned his Bear Award in Cub Scouts when none of the other boys were even close to finishing their requirements.

Then of course she would hear the kids bickering in the background over something really stupid, like who was going to let the dog outside to pee. She would then pipe in about how if they were in school they would learn some real discipline. Is she nuts!?

Next she would say something like, "Well, it seems like everyone is having a lot of fun, but how do you know they're where they should be scholastically?" I'd counter with the results of our latest aptitude tests (I made my children take three in the first year just to have proof that they were learning something). She'd come back saying something like, "Well, that sounds good, but are they *really* learning?"

Before I would start screaming about her lack of confidence in my ability to educate my own children, she's change the subject to the

S word – socialization. "You know," she'd say. "Pulling your shy son out of school really is only going to make things worse. He's manipulated you to get what he wants – to stay home with you." Ouch! Now she was going to guilt me into sending my children back to a dangerous and unproductive public school system that does not respect our morals and values just so he would be away from me all day. That hurt.

I'd counter by listing all of the social activities my children were involved in which filled an entire notebook page, but that didn't help. Each week I'd hang up the phone feeling deflated, disrespected and worse yet – guilty!

If you have someone like that in your life, the best thing to do would be to stop talking with them. Of course, you can't cut off your mother, but you can set some rules. Now, whenever my mother begins talking about all of the things my children are missing out on, I begin reciting a litany of things they get to do that other kids their age don't: volunteer weekly at the soup kitchen; participate in various writing contests; community theater; scouting events; music lessons; playing outside (a lost skill these days); interacting with children and adults of all ages; and more.

I have also begun collecting statistics and newspaper stories about homeschoolers as well as regular school kids and their activities. Nothing shuts up a naysayer faster than whipping out some newspaper clippings about homeschoolers who are completing duel credits at their local community college while finishing high school and apprenticing with a local merchant to see if they like a certain career, and then one reporting on the high suicide and drug rates among public school kids in the area; or the ultra-high teen pregnancy rate in the state; or the high speed accident that killed three irresponsible teens while joyriding at midnight. I don't know a single homeschool teen who can even stay out past 10:30 p.m. The fact is, most homeschooled students are more productive and more responsible; are better able to stand up to peer pressure and have the ability to think and consider consequences more than their public school counterparts.

Does that mean homeschool kids are perfect? Just look around your own house for the answer to that question. Of course not! But more parental involvement, and less reliance on their peers on a daily basis does give homeschool kids a chance to figure out who they are and what they want out of life before being subjected to a lot of peer control.

So, what is the lesson here? Let the naysayers talk all they want. We know the truth. Homeschooling does work. Our kids are smart. Our kids are disciplined and our kids will succeed in life – and in the world! Don't let the outside world's accusations make you feel guilty for not giving complete control of your children's daily upbringing to some outside source. You are the parent; you are in control and yes, you are doing a phenomenal job. So your daughter won't finish her math book this year. Is she progressing? Does she really understand what she's been taught thus far? That is all that really matters.

PENCIL TIP

Nipping Naysayers in the Bud

 Want to stop all of those naysayers from thwarting your attempts at homeschooling? Answer their questions (and counter their opinions) with the real facts about homeschooling:

- **Homeschooling is the single fastest-growing educational trend in the United States.**

- **Nearly 3 million families homeschooled in 2009.**

- **Recent studies show that homes students are more social than their contemporary counterparts. Why? Because they are exposed to a wider variety of people and situations, and are able to learn to get along with a variety of people, making them socially mature and better able to adjust to new situations.**

- **Ninety-five percent of homeschoolers exhibit an adequate comprehension of national and international politics and** government, compared to just 65% of the average adults living in the United States.

- Seventy-one percent of homeschool graduates participate in ongoing community service activities, including politics, compared to 37 percent of adults in similar ages.

- More than 75 percent of homeschool graduates voted in a national or state election within the past five years, compared to only 29 percent of similar U.S. adults.

- Research shows that homeschoolers who have gone to college had no social skill deprivation, exhibited greater leadership skills, demonstrated stronger work ethic and had higher moral values, integral in their college success.

- On average, a homeschooled student outperforms public or private schooled students by as much as 30 to 37 percent in all subjects.

- Homeschooling allows parents to raise their children in a more natural and caring environment.

CHAPTER THREE

SCHOOL, FAMILY, FAITH: BEING ABLE TO FIT IT ALL IN
You Can Do This!
(HOW TO FIT IT ALL IN)

While we are being honest, let me begin by admitting that today is probably not the best day to be writing on the subject of fitting it all in. Here's why.

This is how my day began: I spent the morning cajoling my 8-year-old to focus. That's F-O-C-U-S! Meanwhile, he spent the morning whining that he was tired ... his stomach hurt ... he was hungry ... he was thirsty ... he was bored ... he couldn't remember how to make a cursive e (or g or f or l, for that matter) ... I was mean ... the dog was sad and needed him to play. Well, you get the idea. You name it and it grabbed his attention; except of course, for his schoolwork.

Then my 12-year-old had the audacity to remind me that I have been promising her some one-on-one time to work on a special history project that I assigned weeks ago. It was meant to give us the opportunity to bond. 'When I get your brother started on his next subject," I promised (yet again). "Yeah, right," she mumbled and stomped away.

By lunchtime I had lost my temper and resorted to yelling at my son. Then I lost my temper and yelled at my daughter. Next, I turned on the dog, dragging him outside in a fit of rage when he dared to bark for his breakfast (or was it last night's dinner he still expected?). Finally, I hit rock bottom and called my husband at work to ream him out for leaving wet towels on the bathroom floor. I was frustrated. I was angry. I was exhausted!

By 2 p.m., with my son's work still not even half done and my daughter off on her own (again), I headed to my home office feeling like a complete failure.

This chapter awaited and I was left feeling like a fraud. After all, who am I to encourage other parents to do this when I can't handle the day-to-day frustrations of homeschooling and working myself? I stared at a blank screen for the next several hours, too embarrassed to even write a single word.

At 5:30 p.m. I headed back downstairs to begin supper. It was late again. The kids were both engaged in a game of some sorts when their father walked in. As I rushed to get food on the table before I heard hungry grumbles I watched as my husband reached down to hug each child. Then I heard the inevitable question, "So, how'd school go today?" I held my breath, waiting for a litany of complaints and whines, readying myself to shoot back with my own rhetoric of complaints about irresponsible and ungrateful children when I heard statements like:

"I finished my book three days early!"

"My butterflies broke open their chrysalis!" (Yes, my 8-year-old actually used the word *chrysalis*.)"

"I learned how to mummify a chicken today!"

"Mom says if I keep working hard I can start eighth grade next month and it's only January!"

With a smile my husband turned to me and said, "Guess it was a good day, huh?"

I stood there dumfounded. "Uhh, okay," I managed to choke back through my disbelief. Today was a good day? By all accounts it had been a complete failure. There had been whining. There had been tears and there had been anger. These were none of the things I had dreamed about when I first envisioned homeschooling my children. Yet, in the end, the day had turned out well. The kids had actually learned something and seemed (dare I say it) excited about the process!

It was at that exact moment several hours ago that I realized that yes, I can do this – and so can you! Now, this is no new revelation, but it is one that I find reappearing from time to time as I lose faith in myself along the homeschool journey.

If there are any nuggets of advice I want to pass along before delving into the more practical tips you will need to get through your own hectic days, it is this: Be kind to yourself. I have learned (oftentimes the hard way), that there is no such thing as Superwoman or Supermom. We cannot have it all – especially all at the same time. That means learning a really simple two-letter word: *NO*.

If you are going to survive this homeschool journey, you are going to have to take a tip from my friend Aimee, who has learned the power of saying no – and is trying to teach me. I have often looked at her in awe as she calmly makes her way through each homeschool day. If there is a mom who seems to really love her work as teacher, mom, wife, homemaker, and more, it is Aimee. I asked her once how she manages to fit it all in. Her reply: From September until May, school and family are her first priority. Everything else has to wait. That means very little volunteering at church or in the community, minimal home projects (unless they are emergencies) and even giving up on the vast majority of her special me time with friends during those months. Instead, she concentrates on the kids' schoolwork, daily household chores and staying close to her husband.

Now, when the beginning of May rolls around, Aimee's life takes some dramatic turns. She wraps up the school year on May 1 and then begins remodeling projects, planning trips and outings with friends she hasn't spent much time with during the school year, delivering for Meals on Wheels while other drivers take much-needed vacations and breaks, and heading up a church vacation Bible school program for nearly 400 kids! Her summers are jam-packed with activity and she loves it. This is her time to reconnect with the world and dig in to projects she didn't have time for before.

Aimee will admit that it took her friends and family a few years to understand her need to concentrate on different things during different times of the year, but now that they know how she best operates, they see how productive her type of scheduling can be.

Now, I have not learned how to organize my time and attention like my friend, but I am trying. Still holding down a full-time writing career while homeschooling, I have learned the true meaning of exhaustion. I have learned, however, that to keep my sanity I have had to let a few things go; a spotless house is one of them. When my children left for school at 7 a.m. and did not return until 4 p.m., I had the opportunity to clean once and forget it for the rest of the day. Working from home afforded me the quick moments to throw in a load of laundry and even quick-clean a bathroom during a much-needed break. With no one home to dirty the place, it stayed awesomely beautiful. Not anymore.

The kitchen floor that used to get mopped every day (what was I thinking), now doesn't see a mop until Saturday unless someone vomits on it. Closets that were once alphabetized now struggle to keep from popping their doors open with the stuff crammed haphazardly in there. Our Christmas tree, that for 18 years was always taken down on January 1, this year, stood naked, void of ornaments, lights and I admit, most of its needles, until almost February 1.

Life sure has changed around here since we started to homeschool! Time is more precious than ever and in order to survive I have had to drastically tweak my idea of what I consider to be normal.

Now, let's look at some practical ways that other homeschooling moms have learned how to create their own new sense of normal and build a schedule that does indeed manage to fit it all in ... or at least most of it.

Getting organized

When it comes to getting organized and setting schedules, the homeschooling crowd can be a very eclectic and creative group. For many, the first hurdle to overcome is the daily schedule or to-do list. Before we begin discussing ways in which you can devise your own plan of attack for the day, let's look at a few ways other moms handle their daily responsibilities.

Barbara the Brainstormer

I absolutely love the way my friend Barbara manages her homeschool days – and her life! The problem is that I have never been able to successfully make it work in my own home. I call Barbara "the Brainstormer" because she is always full of ideas and somehow manages to bring most of those ideas into fruition with very little planning on her part. She seems to be able to just think things up and make them happen – no pre-planning required. You've got to love a mom who can manage that without forgetting some important appointment or missing a deadline!

Here is how Barbara plans her typical week: Every Sunday evening she sits down and lists all of the things she would like to accomplish in the coming week. Anything that needs to be scheduled (practices, lessons, doctor's appointments, etc) are always done after 2 p.m. unless it is an emergency, so she never has to think about what may be on the calendar before mid afternoon. She brainstorms her list for the week with things like:

- **study electricity**
- **visit local historic house**
- **memorize two complete poems**
- **build a covered wagon to go with Westward Expansion unit**
- **conduct three science experiments**
- **clean the bathrooms**
- **buy monthly groceries**
- **watch a movie with the family**

As you can see, Barbara's idea of planning is pretty loose, but it works for her. She rarely gathers her materials ahead of time, and almost always completes everything on the list (along with covering her other curriculum areas). A typical school day at her house begins anywhere between 7:30 a.m. and 9 a.m., depending on when everyone gets moving, and ends around 2 p.m. The kids begin with whatever subject grabs their attention the most and the family moves from subject to subject as their mood strikes – as long as they continue to move forward in their studies.

Barbara doesn't seem to stress much over the details and therefore manages her time – and her school day -- in a more leisurely manner. I wish I could be that easygoing, but I'm not. I need a plan and a check-off list. Otherwise nothing would ever get accomplished and I would be a nervous wreck worrying about what I was missing. The lesson here: loose is good, but only if your personality matches that style.

Olive the Organized

Now Olive and I are good friends for a reason: we think alike. Like me, she needs a plan. She takes two weeks every summer to lay out her school year, complete with all assignments on a monthly basis. Then, each Friday night she breaks the next week's assignments down to daily work bites and places it on a calendar for each child to follow. Olive always knows what her children are working on and expects them to meet deadlines. The rest of her life is pretty organized too. She keeps several calendars in her home to accommodate everyone's extra-curricular activities, appointments, school projects, and her own work-related assignments (did I mention she freelances part time too?). Olive admits that her Day-Timer is her best friend and without it (and its lists) she would be lost.

I know the feeling. Desperate to stop feeling so overwhelmed I decided to ditch my own to-do lists a few years ago only to discover things were going undone. I need the structure – and the reminders – of a daily schedule. Like Olive, I need to stay organized in order to stay on track.

Maureen the Military Mom

Not really a military mom (she just acts like one), Maureen runs a tight ship – even a bit too tight for me. The first time I visited this spunky mother of four and noticed all of the timetables and schedules posted on the walls I thought, "Whoa, there is no room for error in this house." Luckily I discovered that this well-organized mom is not a tyrant after all – she is just a harried homeschooler who has found her own way to keep her family and life in better control. Now, I have to admit that her idea of an organized day is way too intense even for me. Maureen can't keep track of anything unless it is written down, therefore she writes down everything. Her daily schedule even includes this item: 7:15 –7:23 brush teeth. Now that's micromanaging! Still, the system seems to work.

Maureen has a master schedule for each week, which includes appointments, chores, activities, etc. She also has a daily work schedule for each member of the family that lists what everyone should be working on during each part of the school day.

One reason Maureen says she has adopted such a rigid schedule is to give her time to spend with each student on the subjects they need the most help in. For instance, while her younger ones are practicing handwriting, spelling or even doing their daily reading, she can work with the others in math, science and history.

Maureen also co-mingles students in as many subjects as possible, like health, geography, local history, civics, current events and so on. This allows her more time to work independently with her children in the areas in which they need the most direction. By keeping everyone on a strict time schedule, she knows she will have the time and attention to focus on specific tasks with specific children at a given point. "Otherwise," she admits, "the day gets away from me and someone doesn't get the help or attention they deserve. Our homeschool may seem too regimented for many folks, but at least I know with a well-laid plan no one is getting lost in the shuffle. Plus, the laundry actually manages to get done before we run out of clean underwear!"

Hattie the Haphazard

Now, on the other end of the organizational spectrum is my other friend, Hattie. People like Maureen drive her crazy. She doesn't even own a calendar, let alone a day planner. When it comes time to pull together her end-of-the-year portfolio for the local school district, she scrambles to remember what her kids did and when. She knows they have completed all of the required work (and days), but just can't prove it. May is always a struggle for this ultra-laid-back mom. It is not unusual for her to call me at the 11th hour and ask something like, "Do you remember when we went to the planetarium and what book did I use in our study of insects?" Somehow I always manage to remember what her kids did. Why can't I do the same for my own?

Hattie's life looks a bit haphazard to the outside world. Her family unschools, a more innovative approach to home education. What does unschooling mean? Basically, it allows students to work on certain subjects and topics when the kids show an interest – and not before. If her youngest son Jon doesn't feel like reading for a week, he doesn't. Hattie feels that to force him to read will take the joy out of it and if she finds books that interest him he will delve in without being forced to comply with set rules regarding subjects and classes. Days and sometimes even weeks go by without a science class in this household, followed by intense studies in an area of interest her kids discover. For instance, her daughter Kala spent three months last fall learning everything she could about the Civil War. Honestly, there is not an aspect of the Civil War this 15-year-old does not know. During that time, however, science took a back seat. When spring rolled around and her interest in everything Civil War began to fade, Kala turned her interest to the outdoors. Suddenly birding was her new passion and she began tracking flight and migration patterns of birds throughout the world. Again her interests dictated her school day.

Hattie insists that this eclectic and haphazard approach to learning has really paid off. Her two oldest children who are now in college seem to be more well- rounded than most of their college counterparts.

For this mom, flexibility is the key to surviving her day. If the dishes are all dirty, Hattie doesn't worry – she pulls out paper plates. If her youngest can't spell aardvark, she doesn't sweat it. Hattie teaches him how to use the spellchecker on the computer.

Life is an adventure and this family sets sail on a new one almost continuously. While not the ideal way for some to homeschool, this eclectic approach works very well for this unique family.

Sally the Spiritual

While each of the moms described above began homeschooling (at least in part) due to a real need to provide their children with a more spiritual upbringing and educational life, no one has been able to incorporate her religious values and strengths into her homeschool quite like Sally. This very even-tempered mom rarely sweats the big stuff and never worries about the small things that may disrupt her school day. Instead, she relies on God the Father to guide her through each obstacle, always keeping His master plan in focus.

"I begin each morning with fervent prayer that the Lord God Almighty will lead each of my children in the direction He chooses for that day. We may have a class schedule on paper, but if someone expresses a more urgent spiritual question or need, we are apt to stop everything and address it," she explains. "For instance, when my 9-year-old saw the devastation on the news about Haiti last winter, he wanted to do something. So we immediately began to pray about the situation and ended up volunteering at a local emergency agency, packing relief boxes for the Haitians for two weeks. We didn't get a lot of formal work done during that time, but my children learned the importance of caring for others. Plus, they learned more about the country and peoples of Haiti than they ever would have from a book."

"Certainly we want our children to get a good education for life, but my husband and I also strive to give them a Godly education that will serve Him throughout their lives. That is why we allow God to lead our homeschool in every way; through the books we read; the subjects we cover; the curriculum we choose; the topics we discuss and so on."

For Sally, that means intertwining Godly things into every subject. For instance, as her children learn world history, they also learn about life in Bible times and can begin to see why people acted and thought the way they did, when comparing a secular and Christian worldview.

"It can be a unique way to teach all subjects to our children but it works well to augment our entire philosophy of life," she adds. "I could not imagine my children learning any other way."

Figuring out what works best for you and yours

I do not share these different approaches to make you choose one or to feel guilty if your approach does not fit any of these specialty molds. If there is one thing that homeschooling parents must come to grips with, it is that there is no right (or wrong) way to homeschool. There is only your way. Personally, I have had a hard time coming to grips with this reality.

I began my own homeschool journey trying to recreate school in our home – doesn't everyone? It took about two months to realize that was not going to work. Trying to find a happy medium between my teaching responsibilities and my work responsibilities, we tried a new approach: a three-day schedule. On paper it looked great. We would spend three intense (and very long) days, finishing basically an entire week's worth of schoolwork, with the children working independently the other two days on projects and subjects that interested them most. That would give me two full days (plus weekends) to put in 10 to 12 hours per day of work time.

It should have worked. Except for the fact that even my kids – who are very disciplined and motivated students – could not find things to occupy themselves for two entire days each week on their own. They needed help. They could not find supplies. They got lonely and bored and then they started to bicker. My peaceful workdays turned into non-stop questions, complaints and problems. We soon went back to regular school hours.

Then I decided to structure the entire school day around 40-minute classes. That worked fine until my son repeatedly got finished early and moved onto his next class, only to get finished before lunchtime while his sister labored over her work until mid-afternoon. Another failure.

Next, I became more flexible (yes, me, the queen of inflexibility). Now I took a tip from Barbara and wrote out a week's worth of assignments. When the kids finished they were done for the week. No set timetables. No pressure. Now, this worked well for my daughter, who is much better at pacing herself, but not my son, who would work like crazy for two days so he could have a five-day break from school. When I started to add things to his list, he balked, saying it wasn't fair that he should do twice the work as his sister just because he was faster. Again, failure.

This year we are going to try a more varied approach. We are going back to the 40-minute class idea, but this time I will have extra project ideas, worksheets and reading assignments, should anyone get finished early. Or they may opt to work on "homework' (that unfinished work from another class) or start a large-scale project in any interest area they choose during this free time. I figure by giving them plenty of choices they will have more control over their school time and remain challenged. I hope they'll even learn some important time management skills.

My goal for this year to is to begin class work at promptly 8 a.m. and finish by 12:30 p.m. We will break for lunch and then the children will have the afternoon free to work on anything they like (no TV or video games though). That will give me from 1 p.m. to 5 p.m. every afternoon to work on my writing assignments, with another hour or two in the evening, and of course weekends to get caught up.

I am taking another cue from Maureen, who makes no scheduled appointments or activities before 2 p.m. Although my afternoons are spent working in my office, I plan on taking one afternoon every week for errands, appointments, and such. If it cannot be done during that time than it will not get done – unless of course it is a true emergency.

The kids and I have also set aside the first Monday of every month as field trip day to give us the freedom to head out into the world and explore in a more leisurely and stress-free manner. This will also be a good time to invite other homeschool friends along for an educational outing. After all, we do not want to stay too organized and isolate ourselves.

But first and foremost I want to become more like Sally, who cares more about the people her children are becoming and less on what subjects they cover and how many pages they can mark off on their portfolio. I want to find her same level of that God is in control and will work it all out. How liberating! I get tired of taking this entire burden on myself and have learned form Sally that I don't have to. There's someone much stronger (and much smarter) who wants to take it from me – and will. All I have to do is hand it over.

CHAPTER FOUR

CREATING A HOMESCHOOLING PLAN FOR YOUR FAMILY

Once you are have figured out what works and doesn't work for your family and are able to free yourself from the guilt associated with homeschooling your kids, it is time to start devising a workable plan that you and your family can follow. Here are some good places to begin:

Step #1:

Figure out what's most important.

Before you can even begin to prioritize your day, week or year, you first have to figure out what is most important to your school, your family and your life. That means making a few key lists. Sorry, but I did say lists (plural). We'll begin with five very general lists first:

- ### List I: Your School Goals for Each Child

  The first list should contain your school-related goals for each child for the coming year. At this point you do not have to be very detailed. Something as simple as listing 1) read one novel per month; 2) finish Algebra I program; 3) study Ancient Civilizations; 4) take a keyboarding class, etc., will do. There will be time later to flesh out these ideas into a quarterly, monthly, weekly or even daily schedule depending on what best fits you (and your children's) personal organizational style. While you are at it, do not forget to list more than your academic goals here; also include your spiritual and growth goals. Education should be more than memorizing facts and figures; it should also include studies to help your children become better people. On your goal list you may include such personal items as teaching younger children how to pray; developing a solid spiritual life, learning the true meaning of compassion, and more.

- ***List II: Your Extra Curricular Activities (clubs, lessons, sports, etc.)***

  Next, list all of the extra-curricular activities each member of the family is involved in. (Be sure to list what day and time of the week practices, games, meetings, etc. are on.) This will include 4-H, scouts, sports, music lessons, art club, your time at the gym, youth group, adult bible study, etc. Anything that requires you or someone in your family to leave home needs to be listed here.

- ***List III: Family, Home and Work Responsibilities***

  This list may become very long depending on how detailed you decide to go here. Start with your family responsibilities, listing everything you do for your family (doctors' appointments, play dates; outings; etc. Next, list your home chores such as laundry, shopping, cleaning, yard work, garden upkeep, caring for aging relatives, and more. Finally, make a list of your job (or career) responsibilities. Maybe you will list specific projects or just a time that you must be at the office such as 3 p.m. to 9 p.m. Monday through Friday. The idea here is to see how much time you spend handling issues within each of these life areas.

- ### List IV: Your Personal Time

Now if it has been awhile since you have taken time for yourself this may seem like a fruitless chore. But, let's face it, there are things you must do for yourself like go to the dentist, make your annual GYN appointment, get your hair colored (Hey, those grays seem to get more plentiful with each passing week!), and so forth. Start with the personal stuff that has to be done, then add some things you would like to have some time for like: reading a new book every month (or every year), reading the paper each morning, or even indulging in a bubble bath once a month. Personally, I added talking to old friends on the telephone to my monthly "for me" schedule. What you add here is up to you – but don't forget spending quality time with your spouse. It can be very easy for busy homeschooling parents to put off spending time together until something happens and they realize they have drifted apart. Don't let business get in the way of your relationship – add time alone to your personal time.

- ***List V: The Fun Stuff***

Everyone needs to have a little fun. Whether that is alone, with friends, with your spouse or with the whole clan, be sure to think about things you want to in the next year, like take a beach vacation, visit Washington D.C. with the kids, go on a romantic getaway, and more. Something as simple as going bowling or building s snowman can be listed if these are things you want to do but never carve out the time for.

Once you have these basic lists done, take a good hard look. The odds are you are thinking, "There's no way I can fit that all in!" Maybe you are right – you can't. Or maybe you just need to learn how to better organize your time.

The next step to figuring out how to establish a workable (and sane) schedule is to cut out any excess baggage. Look for things that you can either delegate (like picking up the dry cleaning – why not ask hubby to do it on his way home from work?), or that can be deleted altogether. Once I really looked at my own schedule I realized that there just was not enough time in our week for each child to go to a separate music lesson. Instead, we found a music teacher that could handle both piano and guitar and booked back-to-back lessons on the same day. I saved the travel time and hassle of schlepping kids to two different places on two different days. Plus we managed to get a multiple student discount! Bonus!

Once you have trimmed away the activities no one really cares about, begin combining and prioritizing those lists. For instance, if you absolutely must get to the grocery store once a week, put that toward the top of you list. But if everyone in your household has enough clothes to get through two weeks without doing laundry, move laundry down to a weekly instead of a daily one. The same goes for housework. If you can get away with a good dusting once a month, so be it. It is more important to spend time working on your son's science project than clearing the furniture of dust anyway.

Once your lists have been prioritized, pull out the items that can be handled on a monthly basis and write them into your calendar. Do the same for all weekly activities. Finally, it is time to tackle the hardest part: that daily schedule. This will include schoolwork, housework, family time, appointments and more. Again, start with the most important things and move down your list until your day is full. Run out of time (and energy) before you have finished that list? It may be time to start cutting out more activities.

Homeschooling families tend to think that they can do two or three times the activities as traditional school families; and oftentimes they can. Not being tied to a school desk and district calendar certainly does open up a whole lot of time to take advantage of some great opportunities. For instance, my friend Audrey takes her children weekly to serve lunch at a local soup kitchen. While it is three to four hours every week that she must juggle their schoolwork around, it is an experience regular school kids never have the time for.

In my case, my daughter uses her homework-free evenings for rehearsals at a local community theater where she often lands a part in an upcoming show. Were she a "normal" school student who had to catch a bus by 7 a.m. and be riddled with two to three hours of homework each night, we would never allow her to spend four to five hours several times a week rehearsing her newest show. Homeschooling has opened up a whole new world to my young actress and I'm thrilled!

That said, we homeschoolers do have the tendency to overbook our children and ourselves. Recognizing the opportunities our children can have we are more apt to say yes than no when a new activity, club or special event is offered. I'm here to warn you: if you are constantly feeling overwhelmed, overworked, frustrated and tired, than you and your kids are doing too much! Scale back, relax and enjoy the freedom that homeschooling can offer. If you allow yourself to get bogged down with too many great opportunities you will soon find yourself in a mad dash to yet another activity, missing out on the most important aspect of homeschooling – spending quality time with your children.

Whether you decide to run your home and your homeschool like Maureen the Military Mom or Hattie the Haphazard (or any of the thousands of homeschool moms in between), doesn't really matter. What matters is that you:

- **Set some realistic goals – choose what you can accomplish and stop trying to do it all.**

- **Devise a schedule or plan to accomplish those goals.**

- **Say no to anything that does not fit within your goals for that particular week, month, or even year – no matter how much people beg for you to change your mind.**

- **Relax and enjoy the process – homeschooling can be fun! Really!**

True, kids get sick, emergencies happen and families seem to get out of whack from time to time. Staying flexible can – and will – help to lighten the load. Remember, 90 percent of what doesn't get done today can wait until tomorrow – or next week. The key to survival is recognizing and handling that other 10 percent.

What if you still have too many things to get done and not enough time? Expert homeschool moms offer these helpful tips.

Step #2:

Combine subjects, classes and lessons.

Trying to teach several children in several grades without combining some classes and lessons can be downright overwhelming – if not impossible. Take a tip from homeschool veterans: teach the kids together as much as possible. That may mean combining certain subjects, giving each child work to do at their own level or it may mean taking a Unit Study approach, which uses one main topic to cover all subject areas.

Let's start with combining children for certain subjects. This can be fairly easy when talking about subjects like health, art, music, geography, spelling, civics; state history and so on. For instance, after noticing that many of her children's spelling lists started to overlap throughout the year, Erin, the mother of four children, took a different approach. She bought a book with the 100 most often misspelled words in the English language and gave the same list of five to ten words to each of her children, despite the fact that their grade levels ranged form second to eighth. "I figured if these were the most commonly misspelled words than it didn't matter how old they were, they needed to learn to spell them correctly." As the children mastered these lists, she began looking for misspellings in their reports and other papers and when she saw patterns among the children, she added them to their spelling lists.

Meghan, who homeschools seven children of varying levels and ages, does some sort of state history unit every year. They go on field trips to local historical buildings and then discuss important people who have contributed to their state. The younger children color pictures of the state bird, tree, flower, etc. while learning what they are, while her older students might write reports about the economy, industry and tourist areas in their state. "They learn together about the place where we live and it makes it much easier on me to be teaching everyone at the same time," Meghan admits.

Some families even combine history and sciences studies, going into more depth with older students while only covering the basics for younger ones. The idea here is to not end up reteaching the same material later in the day (or year) with a different child. Streamlining can take a lot of the work out of a teaching schedule and free up endless hours over the course of a semester.

Unit studies too are very popular among busy homeschooling moms, especially those with multiple students. The key concept of a unit study is to choose one topic of study – let's say the American Revolution –and then wrap all other subjects around that topic. Language Arts would be handled by reading biographies and other books about the era. Science may include a discussion on scientific advances during that period. Math might include covering basic math facts by figuring out how much ammunition would be needed for a certain battle, how many pairs of shoes a soldier might go through during the time period of the war should he march a certain number of miles per day, etc. Colonial cooking, sewing and other activities might be used to reinforce subject areas. A unit study encompasses every subject needed for study during a certain time period. How long you take to cover a certain topic is up to you. Of course, the subject matter can be handled differently by each age group, allowing independence and more in-depth investigation, depending on the students involved in the project.

Depending on your children's ages, interests and your time availability, you can buy pre-packaged unit studies that give you everything you need for the unit or you can create your own. The choice is yours.

Step #3:

Don't reinvent the wheel.

Whenever possible, use someone else's ideas before taking the time to make it up on your own. Buy preplanned curriculum if your budget allows (that can save endless planning time); scour the Internet for project ideas; ask homeschooling friends for ideas; even join a co-op or sign your child up for an outside class if that will end up being easier on you.

Here's another option: turn to your local Christian school for help. Before entering the homeschool community, my children attended a local Christian school. Just because we withdrew them as full-time students did not mean their school journey there had to end. Right now both of my children are involved in a unique (a very inexpensive) homeschool program that allows them to participate in field trips and special classes like music, art, gym, computer, study skills, etc., and join any sports or extracurricular activities they choose. Much like a co-op, the program allows them to interact in a safe and loving environment, while leaving the major courses up to us to handle at home.

Wanting to return for high school, my daughter has agreed to go there as a part-time student, arriving before lunch and staying for three classes. That way she can be with her friends and we can save a bundle in tuition – the best of both worlds.

The Association of Christian Schools International (ACSI) is a big advocate of Christian homeschool education, and is urging its partner schools to offer these types of programs to homeschooling families all over the nation in an attempt to help parents.

Some schools are opening their doors to offer classes and other programs, while others will lend out books and teaching materials to local Christian homeschool families. One friend asked her local Christian school if she could rent some lab equipment for science and they let her borrow everything she needed – for free!

Another homeschool mom reports that she gets brand new sample textbooks from her local Christian school. "I know the curriculum coordinator there and she told me about all of the samples publishers send them to consider buying their books. Since they can't possibly buy new books every year, she just keeps piling the ones mailed to her in a closet and gives them to students who may need a little extra help in certain subjects or to teachers for extra ideas. I convinced her to give them to local homeschool families and she did. Now there are a dozen families benefiting from those books that were only gathering dust before."

The point here is to find someone who has done what you want to do this year and use whatever resources they have put together. Whether it is a curriculum company, a Web site or a friend, someone somewhere ahs done the work for you – so take what they offer and use it!

Step #4:

Turn your kids into independent learners.

Another good way to turn the tide and give yourself more time each day is to churn out independent learners. Children who do not need your constant attention are more responsible and better equipped to handle things in life. Now, I am not advocating handing your children a pile of schoolbooks or hooking them up to a Web-based curriculum and saying "there you are, don't bother me." What I am suggesting is that you teach them how to handle some subjects and topics on their own. Teach them how to research a report and then write and proofread it themselves. Then all you have to do is check for grammatical and structural mistakes, and follow through by reviewing those rules.

I personally learned the benefits of independent learners when my 13-year-old decided she wanted to learn German. Well, I have never spoken a lick of German in my life and neither had anyone in our family. What did we do? Unable to afford the German course offered at the local Community College, we found a computer curriculum that many homeschoolers recommended. I purchased the program with one understanding: if she couldn't figure it all out on her own, she would have to wait to learn this language. Well, this kid, who could not figure out that a full load of laundry contains more than four pieces of clothing, not only figured out that program, but excelled in the class earning a 92 for the semester (thankfully, the program graded all of her work). This year she will begin German II and she is only in eighth grade. Her goal is to CLEP out of German for college when she is 15. Hooray for her independence! Without that gumption and thirst to learn something new, she would have been stuck learning whatever Spanish I could remember from my own high school days – which would have taken about an hour.

This year, we are going to try this same tactic with a novel writing course she is interested in and a life skills class. I certainly wouldn't trust her to teach herself algebra or chemistry, but there are some very interesting scourses she can now take on her own, that I otherwise would never have found the time to teach her.

Step #5:

Delegate, delegate, delegate!

When it comes to household chores, errands and even some schoolwork, delegate responsibilities as much as you can. Home-school moms who have succeeded over the years advise newbie homeschoolers to stop trying to do everything themselves and hand over some of the work. Children can begin handling chores at the youngest of ages. Older children and teens can pretty much handle any type of housework. Spouses can teach classes, cook meals and run errands when necessary. Sometimes you can even delegate teaching duties to siblings. Connie, the mother of eight, often lets her older teens help the little ones on things like handwriting, simple math and other basic projects. While she does not rely on them to "teach" their siblings, she does ask them to check their work and remind the younger members of their one-room schoolroom to move on to the next task when she is too busy to notice their idleness.

Andrea, another homeschooling mom reluctantly admits that after several years of feeling overwhelmed almost daily by the demands of teaching three school-age children and taking care of two young toddlers, she began to accept outside help. "My grandmother had been asking me for years what she could do to help out. She'd seen my frustration and really admired my tenacity of trying to keep up a house, a family and a homeschool and really did want to pitch in. Living just a few blocks away she would often pop in during the day to watch over the little ones while I tried to do science experiments or tackle algebra with my older ones. Finally, one day when she asked what she could do to help, I gave up and said, "Gran, I hate to ask, but if you could just fold the clothes in the dryer I would be forever grateful. Well, that sweet woman now comes by every Wednesday to fold clothes. It doesn't matter if there are two loads or 20 piled in our laundry room, she faithfully (and cheerfully) folds anything left for her. I can't tell you what a relief taking that one job off my plate has been. Since she started helping out, I have also taught all of the children how to put away their own clothes, so now all I have to do is get it washed and dried and my job is done. It's helped make my days so much easier to handle just knowing that everyone is wearing clean underwear!"

If you can't delegate jobs, ask for help or hire them out (barter if you have to). Jenn, a mother of three admits that she had always dreamed of having someone come in and clean her house – not every week mind you, maybe just once a month. But there was no way her family could afford such a luxury. Then she met Melanie. She had just started her own cleaning service and was getting more than enough calls to keep busy. The problem is that her 4-year-old got out of preschool at 11:30 a.m., which didn't give her much time to get more than one house done each day. Since Jenn lived just one block from the preschool and had her own 3-year-old to care for, she asked Melanie if she would be up for a trade. Jenn would pick up her child Monday, Wednesday and Friday from preschool and feed her lunch, and put her down for an afternoon nap. That would give Melanie until about 4 p.m. to clean houses three days a week. In return Melanie would give Jenn's house a good scrubbing once a month. The two have been bartering for almost a year and absolutely love the arrangement.

When it comes to lightening your load, be creative. You may be surprised at how many ways you can find others willing to take up some of the slack.

Step #6:

Take some time out for yourself.

It may sound odd to tell someone who is trying to find more time in her day to handle a packed schedule to squeeze time out for herself. We'll talk more about this in the coming chapters, but consider how much more productive you are when you are feeling good, have a good night's sleep and have been eating properly. Now consider how much better you would feel physically and emotionally if you took some time out each and every day to recharge, rejuvenate and refocus. For me that means walking the dog at 7 a.m. every morning and 7 p.m. every night. OK, so I'm still multitasking, but honestly, walking the dog really helps to clear my head. I'm sure my neighbors think I'm the crazy lady down the street who talks to herself incessantly while walking her pooch – and I guess I am. Those 30 minutes twice a day give me the chance to escape the noise and commotion of my house, get some fresh air and just think. Sometimes it is just the break I need to figure out the solution to a problem, or it gives me enough space to see why my son is so frustrated with a certain subject or worksheet. Other times, it's just a way for me to not think about anything at all, but to just *be*.

Sample Schedules

Not sure how to make up a daily work schedule? Here are some my friends and I use to give you an idea of how some of us manage our time. Of course, yours can be as detailed (or not!) as you like:

WEEKLY PLANNER		Student:	Justin	Date:	May 17-21, 2010
Subjects/ Days	MONDAY	TUESDAY	WEDNESDAY	THURSDAY	FRIDAY
MATH	Lesson 14-3 fractions	Lesson 14-4	Lesson 14-5	Worksheets & Review	Chapter Test
	x				
SCIENCE	electricity	electricity	experiments	experiments	unit test
		technology video		chapter review	
HISTORY	Lewis & Clark	Lewis & Clark	Lewis & Clark	Lewis & Clark	Lewis & Clark
		carve boat	carve boat	boat	boat
		mapping			
L/A	reading	worksheets	worksheets	worksheets	worksheets
	spelling words	reading	reading	reading	reading
	grammar workbook	spelling words	current event	grammar review	

CIVICS	presidents	presidents	presidents	presidents	presidents
				x	
PA HISTORY	famous landmarks	famous landmarksx	famous landmarks	tourism	tourism
BIBLE	Proverbs	Proverbs	Proverbs	Proverbs	verse Test
		verse	devotion	verse	proverbs
	devotion	x	verse	devotion	devotion
HEALTH	bike safety	water safety	pedestrian safety	germs	germs
GEOGRPAHY	Lewis & Clark Maps		Lewis & Clark maps	Lewis & Clark maps	
GERMAN	Rosetta Stone	Rosetta	Rosetta	Rosetta	Rosetta
COMPUTER	x	x	x	x	x
Time Management	workbook pgs. 52-60	x	workbook pages 61-75	x	workbook pgs 76-82
	x		x	x	x
GYM	ride bike	Little League	walk dog	walk dog	Little League
ART	x	x	famous artists	x	x
MUSIC	guitar	guitar	guitar	guitar	guitar lesson

Sample #2:

What we want to accomplish this week:

- read one book

- do unit study on electricity

- complete five lessons in grammar book

- fractions

- study spelling words

- learn one Bible verse

- map out Lewis and Clark travels

- carve a boat like the one used by the Lewis and Clark Expedition

- finish Chapter 5 of history handbook (Lewis and Clark)

- do six German lessons in Rosetta Stone

- learn about one artist

- finish Chapter 4 of time management book

- practice guitar 30 minutes per day

Sample #3:

8:00 – 8:15 –   family devotions

8:20-8:45 –   math

8:50-9:50 –   reading

9:55-10:30 –   science class/
experiments

10:30-10:45 –   snack and break

10:45- 11:20 –   history/project

11:30-12:00 –   Rosetta stone (German)

12:00-12:30 –   lunch

12:35-1:00 –   art/music/gym

1:05-1:45 –   grammar/spelling/
handwriting/essays/etc.

2:00-2:30 –   geography/Penn.
history/time management

CHAPTER FIVE

HOMESCHOOLING AWAY FROM HOME : HOW FIELD TRIPS AND OTHER ACTIVITIES CAN BENEFIT YOUR KIDS (AND YOU)

The whining ... the bickering ... the complaining ... it just wouldn't stop. Hour after hour, day after day. We were all starting to drive one another crazy. It was January and the kids had lost all of their focus (and me too, for that matter). It just seemed that we never regained our momentum after a two-week Christmas break.

The kids were constantly fighting, I was on edge and my husband was loudly expressing his dissatisfaction at the lack of focus (and work) happening around our homeschool table each day. It was time to buckle down and get back to some real work, he'd yell. But I knew yelling was not the answer. Before we could get things rolling smoothly again I first had to pinpoint the problem causing such chaos in our classroom.

Maybe, I thought, I had worked them too hard at the beginning of the year. We began our new school year on August 30th and had diligently worked a pretty strict schedule from 8 a.m. to 1 p.m. each day. If we stayed the course, both children would finish up their entire curriculum for the year by March 1st, leaving us several months to dig into some personal interest-type subjects and projects. But, had we overdone it? Were my kids just burnt out?

I decided to give them a surprise winter break for one week to give everyone a chance to relax, regroup and refocus. Although we had taken time off for the holidays we had packed it full of other responsibilities, chores and outings. This break was meant to be relaxing. It wasn't and it did not help – as a matter of fact, things got worse. With no structure that week, everyone's tempers and frustration levels rose even higher. They weren't over-stimulated; they were under-stimulated.

That's when I thought maybe it was simply just a case of the winter doldrums. After all, the East was experiencing its worst winter in 100 years and we had been snowed in a lot since Christmas. That's when it hit me – we weren't bored with school –we were bored with ourselves! It had been at least six weeks since we'd been anywhere. Our life had become an isolated cocoon of home, school and one another. That's enough to drive even the closest family apart.

The answer to our dilemma? Get outside and get around some different faces! That began with a few phone calls to some nearby homeschool friends who agreed that they, too, needed some real human interaction. Since the roads were snow covered (yet again), we decided to meet halfway between our two residences for a play date in a snow-filled field. Even though we were all tired of the snow by then, it was refreshing to spend time building forts and such with someone besides one another.

The next day things went a bit smoother around our house as everyone settled in for a morning of schoolwork. At noon, I rang the school bell (a good 90 minutes early) and told everyone to get their boots and coats on – we were going on a field trip! And we did – to the local library for story time. We hadn't done that since the kids were little and they giggled and laughed as the librarian read Dr. Seuss to the five kids who dared to trek out into the winter winds for a few moments. Even though they were years past the story time cut-off date to participate, the librarian was so thrilled to have anyone present she didn't seem to mind the unusual intrusion.

In January, I realized that getting out of the house was just as important to a successful school day as the best curriculum, the most interesting lessons and the most organized schedules. Sometimes the only way for both student and teacher to get through another day is to get out!

Now my family schedules at least one adventure outside of the house every week – sometimes many more! But that doesn't mean you have to plan a lot of organized, expensive or far-away outings. Finding adventure outside your back door can be very easy (and low-key). Let's talk about a few options for you and your kids.

Think back to your own school days as a child. Were you always focused and eager to move on to the next lesson? Be honest now.

The fact is, even kids who attend traditional school can get tired with their surroundings and their classmates. But they have a big advantage compared to their homeschool counterparts: they get to leave each afternoon and head home to a new environment and a different set of people.

When you homeschool, you really are stuck with one another 24/7. That's is not necessarily a bad thing. After all, being together is one of the reasons why many families opt for this method of education in the first place. The problem is, too much together time with little or no outside interaction can lead to boredom, frustration and even revolt!

So, what can a creative Mom do to dull the homeschool doldrums (which, by the way, can creep up any time during the year – not just the winter months)? The best thing you can do is pack up the kids and head out the door and away from home several times per week. This does not have to mean planning elaborate field trips or educational outings. Sometimes adventures away from home are as simple as volunteering at the local soup kitchen, heading to the library for some new reading material, getting together with other homeschool friends for lunch, joining a club or even taking a music lesson. What you do is up to your personal time restraints, interests and, of course, budget. The point here is to actually get up and get out!

Short on adventure ideas? Here are a few boredom-busters (for both parent and child) to help jumpstart the flow of your creative juices:

Extra-curricular activities for the kids

For some families, homeschooling opens up a whole new world of extracurricular opportunities. Homeschooling affords most students a lot of extra time to spend cultivating new interests, hobbies, friendships, skills and more.

It has been estimated that the average public and private school student spends as little as 10 hours a week to pursue outside interests, compared to the 25 to 35 hours per week enjoyed by the normal homeschool student.

Why the big difference? Consider the time traditional brick and mortar students spend on the bus going to and from school (the average is 1.5 hours per day); time spent in the classroom (6.5 hours) and time spent on homework (2 to 3 hours). Add in the time needed for meals, family togetherness and chores, and the traditional student doesn't have much left over.

Now look at the average homeschool student who spends only three to six hours per day in the classroom, with no homework or travel time to account for. Factor in family time, meals and appropriate sleep, and these industrious students have anywhere from seven to 11 hours per day to pursue other interests and socialize with friends.

For many homeschoolers, this time is well spent on a number of these important activities:

- **clubs** (scouts, 4H, rocketry, reading clubs, etc)

- **part-time jobs** (even the youngest homeschoolers often do simple jobs like babysitting, pet-sitting, car washing, lawn care, cleaning, etc. for friends and neighbors

- **private lessons** (learning to play a variety of musical instruments is very popular among the homeschool crowd)

- **theater** (from acting, singing, lights, sound and costumes, many homeschool students become active in their hometown community theater as a way to learn the craft as well as interact with people of all ages)

- **volunteering** (with more time than the average teen, many homeschoolers offer their services at local retirement homes, hospitals, public service organizations, soup kitchens, food pantries, churches and more)

- **Co-ops** are also a popular way for homeschool students to interact socially with other kids their age

- **Sports** are very popular among homeschool students who have more time for practice, games, etc.

- **Discussion groups** are another option for older students who may invest time in book clubs, social clubs, writing critique groups, and even political organizations

- **Sunday School**, Awanas, Pioneer Girls and youth group activities

Field trips

What do kids remember most about their school days? It isn't what words were on their fourth grade spelling lists or even what math problems they learned to master. Most kids describe their favorite teacher, the cool science experiments that went awry during biology or chemistry, and of course their favorite field trips, when citing school memories years down the line.

From the excitement of boarding the bus (especially for us that walked to school every day), to the fun of getting outside of the school for a trip into the "real world," field trips have always been a favorite among schoolchildren.

Now, consider the time restraints placed upon teachers trying to plan pertinent and interesting outings for their students. Or, consider the hassle of finding activities within a one-hour drive that 30 to 75 students with different interests will enjoy – and learn from. Think how fun field trips are for traditional students under these restraints; now consider the possibilities for your own students, free of time limits, school rules and more!

Field trips for homeschoolers are de-signed specifically to match their own personal interests and distinct study areas. What fun! One of the biggest advantages of homeschooling is the ability to pack up and head out on an adventure whenever you and your students want – and need to. You can opt for a one-hour trip to the local park on a whim, or you can plan a more intense day-long excursion or even a weekend or weeklong adventure. The choice is yours!

Adventure learning and homeschooling just seem to go together, so don't miss out on some great opportunities to realty dig into your studies in a more hands-on and unique manner. Far too many homeschooling parents try to conform to a more traditional school setting and miss out on some great ways to not only entice their children to learn, but also to get out and have some real fun together! Going on an adventure out of the house does not have to be hard to plan or implement. Actually, it can be as simple or as involved as you want – and have time for.

Here are just a few more ideas from other homeschooling parents on how to break the monotony of their school day and bring some fun and excitement to learning through field trips:

Going on a nature walk

Whether you head out into your neighborhood or trek through a local park doesn't matter. Nature walks are a great way to change the scenery of your day and learn a few things too. For an even better experience, look for nature centers, bird sanctuaries and other trails in your area. My hometown features several centers that not only offer a myriad of nature-related activities, but also offer free programs for families, as well as complete field trip and study units for a minimal fee. Our family has used these programs many times to supplement our studies or just delve into a new area of interest. While interested in birds, my 8-year-old son spent some time volunteering at a local bird sanctuary filling bird feeders and recording the birds he saw. It was a wonderful way to fuel his budding interest in birding and supplement our unit study on birds. State parks are also a wonderful resource for nature studies, often offering free ranger programs for kids.

Scouting out historical sites

Every county and state has a wealth of historical sites to explore and visit. Many are free; others offer low-cost options. Some states even offer an annual pass offering discount rates to the sites in their state. They're great for exploration, and they augment our studies in local and state history, science and American history. A free program on beekeeping helped us to put our study of bees into real-life perspective, and a maple-sugaring program was fascinating to everyone in our homeschool group from ages 4 to 65! One family I know uses local historical sites as their only state history program, visiting a new site each month. Another friend in our co-op has turned these visits into a real study of the Civil War, choosing only the local historical sites that represent that era. I met another homeschool family during an outing that actually volunteers at a local historic home offering tours and learning how to demonstrate different skills from the colonial era. Needless to say, these children are learning more than how to cook with a beehive oven or how to make a broom by hand. They are learning some important lessons on the hardships of our forefathers, as well as how to speak in front of a group and make a topic interesting for an audience.

Visiting local factories, businesses and community service agencies

One look around your community and you can find enough places to visit weekly for years. Living in a rural area just one hour outside of a major city has given my family more opportunities than most, but I am a firm believer that even the smallest village offers more field trip opportunities than you may realize. First, check with your local service agencies for a tour. This may include:

- **hospital**
- **police station**
- **fire station**
- **ambulance hub**
- **911 call center**
- **soup kitchen/food pantry**
- **EMT training center**
- **county courthouse**
- **state capitol**
- **municipal offices** (a great way to learn about how local government works)
- **state representative's office**

While there, don't just go on a tour; ask about other learning opportunities that may be available. While touring our local emergency room, I asked about other programs offered at the hospital and discovered that they offered a low-cost CPR and first aid course for teenagers. Not only did my daughter get some great training there, but she also clocked enough hours for half a year of health credit.

At the fire station, my children were shown all of the equipment, learned what life as a firefighter is like, and participated in a fire safety course. This hands-on class was a fun and interesting way to learn the same safety stuff I had been trying to teach them for years.

Local businesses, too, are a great place to turn for field trip ideas. Here are just a few of the places homeschoolers have reported visiting:

- **McDonald's** (for a kitchen tour)

- **Pizza Hut** (some let the kids actually make their own pizza)

- **banks** (while the kids love getting to see inside of the vault and how the bank works, some guides will actually do a mini-money lesson on savings, loans, etc. if requested)

- **coffee shop**

- **flower shop**

- **greenhouse**

- **farm**

- **grocery store** (this can be a really fun trip, especially if your local grocer takes you on a tour of each department)

- **ice cream parlor**

- **pharmacy**

- **dentist**

- **veterinarian clinic**

- **bookstore**

- **library** (you may be a regular visitor of the library, but have you ever had the chance to find out how it really works?)

Local museums and gardens are also a good place for field trips. True, visiting museums can get pricey, so be sure to check out the cost of family memberships (especially for places you may like to revisit). Also, ask about reciprocal memberships that allow you to visit other local attractions and museums for free (or a reduced rate). For instance, a membership at the Franklin Institute in Philadelphia also gives the holder the chance to visit some smaller local science museums for free.

Another option here is buying a family membership at an out-of-area science museum, zoo or aquarium that can be used in a reciprocal manner back home. Just check first, as some places will not allow you to do this.

My family has belonged to s small science museum for years now (we visited it on vacation when the kids were really small) for the low fee of only $45. Although we have only visited that particular museum once, that annual membership gets us into about a dozen other museums within driving distance of our home – for free! Now, that's a deal!

Some families split the price of a family membership and then share it (although that does require you to travel together as a group), or they look into volunteer opportunities at a site to barter free tickets. Karen and her family helped clean cages at their local zoo and not only got a unique backstage look at the zoo, but were awarded free day passes for another visit.

Another great avenue to explore is local gardens and botanical areas of interest. They often offer field trip programs (either free or at a very low cost). If not, they can still be a fun place to visit.

One note about museums: check to see if they offer any free or discount days during the week. Many offer specials during their slowest times of the week, month or year. By planning your trips around these specialty dates, you can save a bundle on admission costs.

BONUS FIELD TRIP TIP #1:

Whenever visiting any attraction, be sure to tell the people at the front desk that you are homeschooling. You may be surprised to discover that they offer special programs, packets and even lesson plans to educators pertaining to your visit. I happily discovered this trick while chatting with a Park Ranger at Valley Forge National Park in Pennsylvania. Once she learned that we were visiting for school she handed me a detailed lesson plan for the day; specialty teacher tour guide; student booklet; as well as a full length DVD to take home and use later in the classroom. That resource alone was worth the visit! Since then I have asked at every place we visit and have been thrilled to learn that many places offer many extra educational services and classroom aides to homeschooling families. When they don't, the people at the front desk will often call a specialty tour guide to come take us on a personal tour or answer school-related questions. Of course, it is always best (and more polite) to call ahead to ask for these types of services, but if they are offered take advantage of them when you can!

BONUS FIELD TRIP TIP #2:

Many Christian schools offer field trip opportunities to homeschoolers, so be sure to ask. In my area, we signed up for field trip opportunities through our local Christian school for a very small fee. This not only gives our kids the chance to get out of our home classroom once in a while, but also to spend time with kids their own age. The program also allows my children to attend art, music and Bible classes, and participate in organized sports and other activities and clubs at the school. We have found this to be a great way for our kids to interact in a "real" school environment. Some public schools offer similar programs for those who are interested.

PENCIL TIP

The Benefits of Virtual Field Trips

Sometimes it just is not possible to head out the door for a real live field trip. That's when virtual field trips can come in handy. Where we live, the winters can get pretty harrowing, leaving us stranded for weeks at a time, unable to go farther than the grocery store. When cabin fever sets in and the roads are too icy to travel, I plug into a virtual field trip, giving us all the chance to visit factories, museums, parks and other great sites all over the world! No traveling; no souvenirs, no cost and no hassle. Now that is what I call a great day out (or in)! Virtual field trips run the gamut of boring lectures with very little student interaction to very well-developed, interactive trips that not only show students a new place, invention or topic, but also let them interact with the site as well. Be sure to test drive any field trip before getting your kids all excited. We have experienced a few that were real busts

– but we have also gone on some awesome adventures.

Want to find a few good places to visit via your home computer? Here are some of the best virtual field trip finders on the Internet:

www.whitehousehistory.org

This site offers a great virtual tour of the White House, as well as interactive games and lessons for kids and full printable lesson plans for teachers.

www.360parks.com

While the site itself does not offer free virtual tours, it does offer the opportunity to buy inexpensive DVDs that feature 360-degree panoramic views of all of the nation's national parks and many historical monuments. It's a great resource to have on hand when studying our nations national parks and services. Prices average about $15 to $30 depending on the DVD.

www.geomaps.wr.usgs.gov/parks/project

A free look at the geology of the nation's national parks

www.nasa.gov

The official Web site of NASA, students can find all sorts of space exploration activities, information and virtual tours here.

www.tramline.com

This site offers links to hundreds of different online field trips ranging from a tour of the rainforest and ocean, to local factories and even the inside of a tornado! Lesson plans, discussions and interactive games are also available with some field trips.

www.techtrekers.com

Offering a full range of field trip opportunities, Tech Trekers allows students and teachers the chance to visit all sorts of interesting places and learn about a multitude of topics. From the inside of a beehive to a dairy farm, students can visit just about anyplace in the world through this versatile site.

www.simplek12.com

This is another great site for links to a myriad of virtual field trip sites.

www.hud.gov/kids/field1

This site takes kids on a different virtual field trip in their community each month.

www.kshs.org/teachers/fieldtrips/ theme/politics.htm

This site offers a variety of politically based field trips within the state of Kansas.

www.fieldtripfactory.com

Check out this free online resource for teaching children at home. The field trip factory notifies you of specific touring options during the school year.

www.nps.gov

This site is an indispensible touring guide that takes students on tours of the nation's art and science museums, historical sites, national parks, monuments and more. It's a one-stop shop for historical, science and art-related field trips offered by the government.

This is just a small sampling of what is available on the Web, so be sure to take a look at a variety of field trip options through your favorite search engine. Type in the words "field trips" or "virtual field trips" or "online educational trips" or just type in your area of interest and see what pops up.

When looking for an online tour or field trip, consider these important tips:

- **Age Appropriateness**

Not every virtual field trip is appropriate or even interesting for every age group and/or grade level. Be sure that the tours and trips you schedule offer information your children can understand and learn from.

- **The Type of Tour Offered**

Some virtual field trips offer a multi-sensory "tour" of the topic, while others are in lecture format and still others offer graphs and pictures but require the child to do a lot of independent reading. Check to make sure that the tours you choose offer the right mix of presentations to best suit your children's interest levels.

- **Hands-On Activities**

If your children like to play games, make online choices and use a lot of hands-on activities programs. Then be sure that the virtual tours you choose offer just that. Otherwise, your children might get bored and turn away from the screen.

- **Multi-Media Presentation Options**

Not every virtual tour offers a lot of multi-media action. Some are little more than a lot of pictures and views of a specific topic. Others showcase graphs, lists and other stand-alone manipulative. Choose the types of multi-media presentations your children respond to best and then pick virtual field trips offering those.

- **Length**

Varying in length from just a few minutes to several hours, virtual field trips can be as long or as short as you want and your children like.

- **Complexity of the Subject**

Again, some topics lend themselves to a very complex dissuasion or overview, others do not. Depending on your children's age, grade and interest level, you may want to look for more in-depth tours.

- **Topics of Interest**

With literally thousands of topics to choose from, your children will never get bored when looking for virtual field trips to explore online. Topics range from geology, geography and world cultures, to art, science and government.

Planning Those Bigger Trips

Of course adventure away from home can take on a much grander scale if your family so chooses. For instance, I know one homeschooling family who took six weeks and travelled throughout Europe during their study of world history and cultures. They were lucky in two respects:

1. The father of this family was self-employed, which afforded him the opportunity to take such a long leave of absence form work.

2. The entire family had been very involved with their church's mission program for years, writing regularly to missionaries and supporting them financially. One way they managed to keep their travelling expenses low was to coordinate their stops in each country with a missionary family with whom they could stay for a few days without lodging or food costs. This is the only thing that made the trip financially possible.

Other families I have spoken with report doing similar trips by either doing mission work while there or visiting family members overseas when available. Staying in hostels is another good option for families to help keep foreign trip costs down.

For those unable to plan such a large-scale trip on their own (or whose finances can't sustain it), one option is to do short-term mission work. There are dozens of Christian organizations all over the country that plan mission trips and would be happy for you to join in their efforts. Most churches these days also offer oversees and domestic mission trip opportunities too. If your home church does not offer a family-style missions opportunity (or if they are not planning a trip to an area you would like your children to see), then consider calling other churches in the area to see if there are opportunities elsewhere.

Sarah and her family use mission opportunities through local churches to help expand their children's understanding of the world today, different countries' histories, and caring for the world.

"The first year we headed to Belize and were able to see a whole new world. We spent the month preparing for the trip to learn about the people, culture, politics, economy and more about the country. Once there, we were put to work building a school and were able to work side by side with the native peoples. Our entire family (ranging in ages 8 to 45) came home with such a yearning to do (and learn) more about the world we call home. We now work very closely with our church's missions committee, planning a variety of trips that serve all kinds of areas around the globe," she explains.

The Jones family began serving on the short-term missions field after they're oldest had completed an in-depth study on Africa for history class and famous missionaries for Bible class.

"It was like God had planned it all," Janet Jones explained. "Seth was really getting into these studies and then our church announced a mission trip to three points in Africa to help treat AIDS babies in several clinics there. Seth immediately began begging us to let him go. Uncomfortable allowing our 15-year-old to travel so far alone, we decided that our entire family would go. The experience was so rewarding that we now return every year as a family to volunteer for two weeks at one of the clinics. We have learned so much about the people there and the way they live. The surroundings are beautiful and we have been able to go on several excursions throughout the wild, thanks to friends we have made over the years. These trips teach our children more about the world and different cultures than any textbook. Plus, it gives our family a chance to grow closer and appreciate what we have back at home."

Of course, you do not have to travel far away from home in order to do mission work. There are plenty of domestic opportunities also, especially in very rural and very urban settings where much help is needed. From building schools in the Appalachian Mountains to building parks in downtown Chicago, domestic mission opportunities are plentiful, giving kids a chance to learn about their own land and peoples.

Keep in mind though, mission trips are not vacations. They are work trips. Above and beyond the social interaction and academic opportunities, your family will be required to work – and work hard. Still, most families believe that this is also a skill that is worthy of being taught to today's youth.

Another note here: Mission's trips are not cheap (especially when an entire family plans to go). But most people find that asking their church family for support and doing a few fundraisers prior to the trip enables them to secure the necessary funds. "It costs our family close to $10,000 to go on a single one-week trip to Poland every year to work at a church day camp. If it weren't for some creative fundraising ideas from my kids and the help of our church family, we would never be able to do it. But every year God comes through and we find ourselves on that plane," admits Janice, the mother of four. "So, never let the cost thwart your efforts. If God wants you in a certain place at a certain time, it will happen."

While a long foreign trip or a work-related missions trip may not be possible for your family for a variety of reasons, a longer, more local trip may be. Right now my family is planning a cross-country trip to be taken in a couple of years. Why such early planning, you ask? My husband and I agreed that this was a great opportunity to teach the kids a variety of skills: map reading, trip planning, state history, American history, science, etc. We plan on using as many skills as possible while planning this trip.

In the next 12 to 18 months our children will be completely planning and organizing this trip by:

- **Setting our course**

- **Learning about the states we will be visiting, and figuring out which landmarks to stop at during our travels**

- **Figuring out how many miles a day we can travel (with stops)**

- **Choosing places for us to visit and camp along the way**

- **Calculating fuel needs**

- **Figuring out the cost of the trip including gas, food, campsites (lodging), attractions, souvenirs, emergencies, and more**

- **Including two routes (one to get to the West Coast and a different one for our return home)**

- **Listing the things we will need to take care of before our trip in regards to the care and safety of our home, as well as while we are away**

- **Figuring out a plan in regards to someone getting hurt or sick, detours, car emergencies and more.**

As the trip grows closer, the children will have to figure out what to pack for such a long trip as well as devise a plan for raising some of the funds needed for a three-week trip like this. Some of the ideas they have already come up with are: having multiple yard sales; pet-sitting for neighbors when they go on vacation; giving up our normal vacation for the next two years; even giving up one Friday night pizza per month and putting that money aside for the trip.

My 13-year-old also scouted out the locations of the Costco Food Warehouse Clubs along the way to see where we could shop and eat cheap while traveling. (I thought that was a great idea!). "After all, she reminded me, if we shop on Saturdays while all of the sample people are out you won't even have to feed us lunch that day because we can eat for free while you stock up on supplies." What a creative idea!

Still not convinced that you are up to planning a large-scale trip with your family? No worries. Why not just plan a weekend excursion chock-full of fun and educational things to do? That's the beauty of homeschooling – you can plan any type of excursion you want with little regard to school schedules and scheduled days off. If you want to head to the mountains on a Wednesday you can go for it!

BONUS FIELD TRIP TIP #3

When planning field trips, consider the day of the week and month of the year. May and June are typically very busy months for traditional school outings and result in very crowded amusements. On the other hand, if you choose to go somewhere on the first day most students are back in class after a long break (right after summer break, Christmas break, Spring Break, etc.), you are likely to be the only visitors there. This can result in a very relaxing and entertaining visit – plus the people who work there will have much more time to discuss things with your children! Mondays are usually very quiet field trip days, making sites more accessible, while Fridays are very popular, making them more crowded. One benefit of going when other schools do: some places will let you tag along with a school trip and participate with their tour guide – a real bonus sometimes!

As you can plainly see, there are plenty of great opportunities for homeschoolers to enjoy when it comes to getting out of the classroom and enjoying some new adventures. Whether it is taking a class, signing up for private music lessons, going on a cross-country jaunt or just heading out to the park for the day, getting out of the house can be as simple or as complicated as you like. Heck, you can turn just about anything into an educational experience if you think about it. So why limit yourselves to books, workbooks and computer programs for your teaching? Head out into the big world and explore – you will all feel better for the experience – and learn lots too!

CHAPTER SIX

TAKING TIME TO RECONNECT WITH YOUR HUSBAND & HOW YOU CAN WORK TOGETHER TO EASE THE STRESS OF HOMESCHOOLING

It had been three years since my husband and I had a date – a real date. So we hired a babysitter, got dressed up and bought some tickets for a theater production in the city. We were going out! There was only one rule: we could not talk about the kids during our time away with each other. It sounded easy enough. We would soon find out.

We got in the car and he asked for the address to the theater. "Guess it'll take about an hour to get there," he said. "Okay I replied. It will be nice to drive without listening to the bick – –" his glare cut me off. Oops! I'd broken our only rule and we weren't even out of the driveway yet. I smiled and closed my mouth, sentence unfinished. There would be plenty of time to talk.

We drove in silence. About 45 minutes later, my dear husband said, "Hey we made good time."

"Yup," I answered. "A real record."

After finding a parking space near the theater he said these romantic words, "Wasn't that a great space? You won't even have to walk far in those crazy heels!"

That's my man! He's always thinking of me.

Entering the theater I thought, *Thank goodness we don't have to talk in here.*

The show was great, which gave us something to talk about during dinner. Then it was time to head home. Having exhausted our talk about the play while we ate, we endured another silent trip home. As we drove into the driveway, I sighed.

My husband leaned over, "What's wrong, didn't you have a good time?" he asked.

"We don't even have anything to talk about," I fought back the tears. "What happened to the way we used to talk?"

"When?" he asked.

"When we were dating," I answered.

That's when he laughed. "You don't remember, do you? We didn't talk back then either, we just necked in the car."

"Oh," I whispered. He was right. We did do a lot of smooching back then – of course, we talked too!

"I have an idea," he said. "Just for old time's sake, why we go park somewhere quiet?"

"Oh, you!" I smacked him and laughed. "What if we get caught?"

"So what?" he answered. "We're married now. It's not like they can call your dad!"

He was right. So we did the only thing we could do. We backed out of the driveway as quietly as we could. After all, the babysitter was paid up for another hour ...

As parents we sometimes forget the importance of nurturing our relationships with our spouses. More often than not, we tend to put our spouse and his need for attention aside to handle more urgent matters like dirty diapers, a crying infant, bickering siblings and other everyday annoyances. By the time bedtime rolls around and the kids are quiet, we have either fallen asleep on the couch or we set off on trying to finish a project or chore that had been put aside earlier in the day. Where does that leave our spouse? Alone watching TV or sitting up in the bed all by himself.

Why do we so often shove our spouses aside? Because we think they will wait. And for the most part, they do; day after day, and night after night. But, if we aren't careful, we will soon find ourselves drifting apart as everything (and everyone) else in our lives takes precedent over the most important person we know – the one who loves us through it all. That can be really dangerous to a marriage – and a family.

Dedicating time for each other is vital to every marriage, but especially the homeschooling one. Taking full responsibility of your children's education can be an all-encompassing job. Mothers who homeschool often take the brunt of the teaching responsibilities due to the time commitment involved (after all, someone has to work to pay the bills and that is usually Dad), so he is often left a bit out of the loop. If she is not careful, this can lead to resentment on both ends: resentment from her for having to "do it all" and resentment from him because she's constantly taking over and shoving him aside.

One way to avoid frustration and complaints about overburdened schedules and unsupportive spouses is to:

1. Take time out for each other.

2. Share homeschool and home care responsibilities.

3. Accept the unique ways in which your spouse handles the kids, home and chores and school-related activities.

4. Spend time together as a family.

Take time to nurture your relationship

Quality time spent with one's spouse is never wasted. Whether you sit on your porch at night watching the fireflies, going out on a date or just snuggling in bed watching your favorite movie doesn't matter. What matters is taking a time out for (and with) each other.

Nurturing your relationship with your spouse should be a top priority in your home. Without a happy marriage even the best homeschool efforts will fail. One of the best lessons you can give your children is to allow them the privilege to see what true love, compassion, patience and understanding really are. To watch your parents' love grow through the years is a gift few children get to experience these days.

Marriage can be difficult under the best of circumstances. Throw in a houseful of kids, a homeschooling journey, troubled finances and a lack of sleep, and you could be headed for disaster – unless you recognize the need for nurturing each other.

Of course, taking regular time out to spend some moments alone, reconnect and slip in some romance is always good, but don't forget to include some day-to-day actions that tell your spouse how important he is. Try and find at least a few minutes each day to just check in.

Aimee and her husband have a morning ritual where they take just 10 minutes to sip a cup of coffee in bed before he heads off to work. This allows them to touch base with one another at least once during the day and just have a quiet moment to remember how much they love one another. It's a simple thing that takes virtually no time or effort, yet she claims that it has helped them stay close over the years. "Even if an entire day and evening goes by in a rush of activity, we know that we have at least spoken that day. Some couples can go a week without saying two words to one another. That's sad really."

Karen has her own way of touching base with her husband. Understanding that she could let months go by without ever acknowledging his contributions to their family (she admits she often complained about the things he *didn't* do more than acknowledge the things he *did* do), Karen began a weekly ritual of leaving a message on his voice mail at work to thank him for going to work that week. "I just always took it for granted that he should get up every morning and go to work to care for his family. Then it dawned on me that it would be nice to let him know I appreciated the effort. After all, who wants to get out of bed at 6 a.m. every morning and work all day to come home to an ungrateful wife?"

Like these two women, we all need to find simple ways to let our spouses know how much we love, respect, and yes, *acknowledge* what they do for us each and every day. Sometimes that means planning a special meal, or asking a friend to watch your kids for the evening so you can spend time alone. Other times it means saying "thank you" or "great job" when he finally hangs up his wet towel or unloads the dishwasher before going to bed at night.

Take time on a regular basis to tell your spouse how you feel. Show them how much they are loved and needed. And express your gratitude for both the big and small things he does to help you and the family.

Of course, the key to nurturing any relationship is having some fun together. Go for a walk. Play a game. Do something new and different. Just find some ways to laugh and enjoy each other's company in a stress-free environment. Some couples like to golf together. Others play tennis. Jill and Brian play "Scrabble" on Saturday afternoons, and Rachel and Mike ride their bikes through town.

Another important way some couples nurture their relationship is to grow closer spiritually. For Kevin and Maddie, adding a prayerful element to their marriage was a must. "From the earliest days in our marriage, we have taken time to pray with (and for) each other," Maddie explains. "You can't pray for each other if you are not connected."

Like many Christian couples, Kevin leads his wife and family in devotions and Bible readings every evening before bed. They discuss specific bible teachings that are pertinent to what is happening within their household that a particular day. Then, privately as a couple, Kevin and Maddie pray for each of their children as well as their own relationship.

Sometimes they even pray for God's guidance in choosing the right homeschool curriculum. "There isn't any aspect of our home and school that we can't (and don't) put in God's hands," says Kevin. "That really is the only way we have been able to survive the hard days."

Want to bring God into your marriage and homeschool? Here are a few suggestions:

- **Study a particular Bible passage or book of the Bible together as a couple.**

- **Attend a couple's Bible Study.**

- **Attend a Christian marriage-enrichment seminar/workshop or retreat.**

- **Pray together regularly.**

- **Attend regular services as a family.**

Sometimes getting back on track (or staying on track) means taking small moments together, and sometimes it means planning a real getaway. Some couples like to plan regular date nights, some plan weekend getaways, and others take a week every year for a private vacation alone. Again, the choice is completely yours.

PENCIL TIP

Learning to Affirm One Another

 Everyone wants (and needs) to know that they are appreciated. Here are a few simple ways to let your spouse know how much you appreciate all he does for you:

- Slip a note or card into his briefcase before he leaves for work.

- Get up early once in a while and make him a hearty breakfast to give him a good start to his day.

- Leave a message on his voice mail telling him you love him.

- Surprise him with a picnic lunch.

- Plan an evening out (or in) – just you and him.

- Send him a special email.

- Say thank you.

- Name three things he's done this week that you appreciate.

- Tell him five things you love most about him.

Sharing homeschool and homecare responsibilities

No matter how big the load, it is always much easier to handle tough jobs when you can share the responsibilities. That includes homeschooling. It is not uncommon for the mother to handle the bulk of the family, home and schooling responsibilities, simply due to the fact that she is the one at home. But that does not mean that her husband shouldn't (or can't) be brought in to help when the burden becomes too heavy.

In many cases, husbands do want to help, but feel as if they are intruding if they try to lighten their wife's load. "I have always loved science," says Chris, "And yearned for years to take on more of the children's science education. Sure, I couldn't hold science classes during the day while they studied their other subjects, but I knew I could handle a few nights a week or a long more in-depth class on Saturday mornings. But I was afraid to ask my wife if I could try. I didn't want to step on her toes or make her feel as if she was doing a poor job. Besides, she is a very organized and scheduled woman and I thought by asking her to bend to my time constraints it would mess up her whole schedule."

Chris went on to explain how, when their 4th child was born, his wife had a hard time coping so he took over both science and math classes for her since they seemed to overwhelm her the most. It didn't take long before she realized how much fun the kids were having with their dad and how easy it seemed for him to develop interesting lesson plans and incorporate several styles of learning into his program.

"She came to me one evening and asked if there was any way I would consider taking over those two classes on a permanent basis. I couldn't believe my ears! She was asking me if I minded doing something I'd wanted to do for three years! I can't believe we wasted so much time and energy trying not to invade each other's space that we almost ended up frustrated and overwhelmed by it all."

Now, Chris says that his wife is happier and more relaxed having two major subjects taken off of her educational plate, and he is able to participate in his children's education in a more tangible and fun way. "I handle math each evening after supper while my wife cleans up the kitchen and puts the little ones down for the night. Saturday mornings are dedicated to long science discussions and experiments, with weekly reading and homework assigned for the normal school day while I am at work."

Like Chris' wife, you may secretly yearn for your husband to help with the children's schoolwork, but feel guilty asking him to take on more responsibilities when he works all day. Don't make the mistake of becoming more and more overwhelmed by your own tasks – and don't fall prey to grumbling and nagging. Instead of insinuating that you need help – ask for it! Be blunt and be decisive. Instead of saying something like, "It sure would be nice if someone helped me grade these papers," plainly ask, "Will you grade some papers for me this evening? I'm a bit behind and could really use the help." You may be surprised by your husband's reaction.

When it comes to getting your spouse to share teaching duties, think about what he has the time, energy and talent for. Ali wasn't any good at higher math and really thought her husband (an engineer) should teach their teenager calculus. "I certainly was qualified," he admits. "But I work a crazy schedule with a lot of late meetings and nighttime phone calls from overseas. Travel, too, can be a problem during some projects. I just didn't feel like I could give my son the structured time a class like that needed. My wife didn't like that. She thought I was throwing all of the work to her when in reality, I just didn't think I could give my son the quality education he deserved. We compromised and signed him up for a calculus course at or local community college."

Ali and Mike learned an important lesson: just because your husband says he can't (or won't) help out, does not mean he does not care. It just may mean he can't do it right now. When that happens, be sure to talk it out clearly so you both completely understand the other's needs and look for a compromise. There is always a compromise.

Mary and Jack had a similar problem. Instead of paying the high cost for an outside science class, Mary handled the bookwork during the day with their daughter, and Jack went over troublesome areas when he got home from work. Plus, he worked on projects and experiments on the weekends. In the end, everyone got what they needed with little frustration.

For Pat and Steve, the answer came in the form of a good friend (a retired English teacher), who agreed to help their daughter with English composition one year when she hit a roadblock neither of her parents could break. "Sometimes it takes an outside person to help too," Pat admits.

Schoolwork is not the only area in which chores can be distributed between parents. Childcare and household duties can too. Sometimes it is actually easier to hand off these responsibilities than actual class work since they can be handled in a more convenient manner. For instance, while math must be taught on a daily basis, scrubbing the bathrooms can be done when your spouse has the time.

Keep in mind that when it comes to taking care of a household, no job is gender specific. True, women may be able to handle certain jobs easier and with more grace than men (and vice versa), but when it comes to tag-teaming the house and kids, getting it done is sometimes better then getting it done perfectly. Strive for completion now and perfection later (when the kids are grown and out on their own).

Fathers can be very good at bathing, feeding and diapering children. They also have a real knack for getting children to bed (and to stay there). So why not let them handle it? Besides helping you out and relieving your stress, it also offers your husband a great opportunity to build relationships with his children.

Household chores can often be delegated to your spouse. My husband, for instance, has taken over all laundry in our house. Now before you begin to think he's perfect (he's not), let me explain. I was trying to find something that he could do and not cause a fuss, so I asked him if he could the laundry on Sundays while watching baseball or football (depending on the sports season). That way he does not have to give up his relaxation time on the weekend or leave the couch for long, he gets to watch all the sports he wants all day, and I don't feel like he is getting away with something, leaving me to all the household chores. So he sits there on Sundays folding the laundry (switching loads during commercials), and the kids put it away. It is a great deal for all of us. See, getting your husband to help out around the house does not have to be another chore – it can actually be a help!

The important thing to remember when trying to delegate chores to your spouse is to find ones that he:

- **can handle** – No one wants to be given chores that are beyond their skill set. If your spouse finds housework too hard to handle, then by all means find something else. It takes a lot of different skills and jobs to run a household, so find jobs that your spouse can handle without getting frustrated.

- **doesn't hate** – After all, how would you like to be told to do something you hate, and then be expected to do it to perfection? Find something that your spouse actually enjoys (like gardening, building, etc) and you just might find those projects getting done!

- **has the time to finish** – Forget repainting the entire house or retiling the bathroom (for now, anyway). Stick to the smaller, more manageable jobs at first. Assigning large-scale jobs that he can't finish in an acceptable time frame will only frustrate you both.

- **is good at** (or at least not lousy at) – Everyone is good at different things. I may stink at painting but I sure can organize a closet! Find the things that your husband is good at and he'll be able to get even more done than you thought he could!

Think about some things you can ask you husband to handle for you. Here are a few samples:

In the classroom

Even if your spouse is too busy or too tired to help teach specific subjects to your children, there are plenty of things he can take care of in regards to the classroom. Choosing curriculum is one of them. Placing the next year's curriculum order can be a big chore for some moms. Personally, this is my favorite part of homeschooling, but one mom I met absolutely hates it. So her husband is the one who scours those catalogues and Web sites looking for the best deals. Let me tell you, this man is great at finding the most innovative and unique books, computer programs and other educational resources!

Many couple's have found that getting away for a weekend once a year to review their student's progress, discuss what works and doesn't work in their homeschool (and home), go over their educational plan and decide on curriculum choices, can be a great way to reconnect and involve each other in the process. By taking just two days to go over everything, both partners are on board for the coming year. This is also a good time to review who will be responsible for which home and school duties for the coming year.

When it comes to making detailed lesson plans, Audrey admitted that she was less than enthusiastic – or timely. After hearing her complain week after week about the hassle of developing a plan, her husband suggested that she write out a detailed lesson plan during the summer for the coming year – something she could more easily follow when things were most hectic.

"Yes, that sounds easy, but who has the time to do that?" she asked. So he did it. Guess what? His plan worked perfectly. He took a few evenings to map out a complete plan for each student in each subject. Typing it into special forms he created on the computer, Audrey could easily move unfinished items to the next week, with the computer pushing everything forward if needed.

Seeing how much more relaxed his wife was, Phil decided to tweak his plan midway through the year by adding materials lists and such at the beginning of each week's lesson plans so that Audrey could put together manipulative and project packs on Sunday afternoon that could be easily grabbed off of a shelf when needed.

"What a blessing," admits Audrey. "Phil's help in keeping me organized and on track has made our school week so much easier. I don't feel so overwhelmed and rushed all of the time. Better yet, he doesn't mind doing it. He says this is an easy way for him to help out and feel like he is part of our children's education without coming home after a long day and actually teaching a class."

Like these wives, you can find things for your husband to do in regards to making your homeschool journey less harrowing. Here are a few basic suggestions:

- **grade papers**
- **review work with students**
- **read aloud to students**
- **organize paperwork**
- **create annual portfolios**
- **file appropriate paperwork with the school district and/or state**
- **create lesson plans**
- **help chose and buy curriculum**
- **clean up classroom**
- **shop for school supplies**
- **put together project packs**

Around the house

When it comes to helping out with home and hearth, there is a lot your husband can do. Just ask Melody. She spent years trying to do everything herself. Before long, her husband didn't even try to help out anymore. Why should he? When he did try to help out, she snarled that he was doing it wrong. When he didn't help, she complained that he made her do everything around the house. But when Melody began homeschooling, she realized that something had to give, so she started giving her husband lists of things she didn't have time to complete on her own. He balked at first, but eventually realized that she was not asking him to take over all of the household chores, just to pinch-hit for her when needed.

Not sure where to get started on involving you own husband with household chores? Here are a few ways to get started. Have him:

- **wash dishes**
- **do laundry**
- **clean bathrooms**
- **dust**
- **sweep**
- **shop for groceries**

- help to precook meals to be used later in the week

- make beds

- bathe children

- read bedtime stories

- take out the trash

- walk the dog

- run errands

- clean up toys and clutter

- mop the floor

- change linens

- clean the garage

- do simple maintenance

Remember though, not to add too much to your husband's plate. Often it is easier to ask him to perform small tasks than large-scale projects. For instance, instead of asking him to reorganize the garage, simply ask him to fill two garbage bags full of trash this weekend. Next week, give him another simple chore. Before you know it, the larger project will be completed.

It is important to remember that when you homeschool, your priorities must shift (or you risk losing your sanity). That often means that tasks take more time to complete. Neither of you may have time for a full spring cleaning with your current responsibilities at home, work and church, so just do what you can handle. That may mean cleaning out the closets one month and scrubbing woodwork another. Sure, your "spring" cleaning may end up taking all year, but it will get done – eventually.

Getting your husband to help may be difficult at first, especially if you are a real taskmaster who wants everything done yesterday – and your way. Be kind, be patient and accept your husband's best (which may not be your idea of perfect – or even correct) and you will all be much more content. Sometimes, you will need to just let things go when there is too much to get done and not enough time to do it. Personally, I used to vacuum my carpets every day; now it only gets done twice a week. The same is true for the kitchen floor. And, you know what? No one has even noticed. (Or at least they haven't had the guts to mention it!)

Accept your spouse's unique way of handling his responsibilities

No one does it like a Mom. That may sound egotistical and stereotypical, but admit it, Mom, that's exactly what you were thinking! Alas, your husband may do things differently, but if you want him to help, you are just going to have to learn to accept that fact – or do it all yourself (gasp!).

Sometimes I wonder how my husband and I ever got together, let alone fell in love and managed to build a family together. We are real opposites; he loves sports and I couldn't care less; he loves to travel and I am a real homebody; he loves the water and I could go an entire summer without dipping my big toe in the pool; he is adventurous and I am NOT; he is a procrastinator and I have everything done days or even weeks before it is due. I even like to pay the bills the day they arrive and he is happy paying them at midnight the day they are due.

As you can imagine, life around our house can get a bit, dare I say, loud, when things begin to go astray. I need him to grade papers and he says he will, and then proceeds to read the newspaper. The newspaper? Come on! Grade the papers!

Lest you think I am exaggerating, let me tell you a story. I had been scouring the flea markets for the perfect picture to hang behind our couch in the living room. We had one there but neither of us liked it. Unable to find one, I went to Target for cleaning supplies. When I checked out their home furnishings department, there it was – exactly what I was looking for! The only problem was that it was not on sale and I never buy anything that is not on sale. As I stood there staring at the picture I'd wanted for so long, something came over me and I put it in my cart.

Worried that I had spent too much and that it wouldn't be right, I decided to tape the receipt to the back of the frame. I figured we'd hang it up for a few days and then decide whether to keep it or not. So I placed the picture against the wall next to couch and asked my husband to please hang it. He said, "OK – in a few minutes."

Well, that few minutes turned into a few days, then a few weeks, then a few months. Finally, frustrated and unhappy, I slid the frame behind the couch. Every once in a while I'd make a sly remark about the picture and he would shrug and say, "I'll get to it." I knew what that meant: I'll get to it in David time – which in reality meant the time warp of time.

Last year, we repainted the living room and when we moved the couch there was that perfect picture. "Oh, I guess I'll hang this now," he said matter-of-factly, as if I had just bought it this week. Let me tell you, the sparks began to fly and I began to scream, venting out all the frustration I had about that picture and every other undone chore he has set in my lap over the years.

"Come on," he said. "It hasn't been that long." So I showed him. I pulled that receipt off of the picture and thrust it at him. "Here," I grunted. The date on the receipt was for four years earlier. "Now call me a nag!"

His eyes got big. His face drained of color. All the nagging and screaming in the world did not make the point that receipt did. "Now," I said. "I understand that you do things differently than me. I want it done yesterday and you are thinking next week, but really, this is a bit excessive isn't it?" Even he had to agree.

So, what's the point of my story? The fact is, our spouses are wired differently than us, especially when it comes to getting things done. Some are procrastinators like my husband, others are more like me, needing to get everything done right away so they are not left with a pile of jobs to do at the end of the week. It is important to recognize your differences and then make concessions for them. But it is also important to find ways to show your spouse when they are being unreasonable. Yelling, screaming and nagging don't accomplish anything (I know, I have tried). Instead, find a more tangible way to show them the importance of getting the job done in a timely manner – likely throwing a dated receipt in his face!

For instance, I may ask my husband to assemble our children's portfolios for the school district, since they come with a legal deadline, while I handle something around the house that needs to get done but can often easily be put aside for later. That way both jobs get done and I am not stressed about either.

Jolee gives her husband a monthly list of projects. She doesn't care when he tackles them as long as the entire list is finished by the last day of the month.

April doesn't use that tactic – it overwhelms her spouse. Instead, she gives him regular jobs to complete. He grades papers Friday night, cleans the downstairs bathroom Saturday morning, and picks up all of the kids' leftover toys, shoes, etc. every night before he heads up to bed.

Janice just asks her husband to do two things each morning: make their bed and hang up the wet towels in the bathroom. "If he does those two things, I don't feel so much like I'm being taken advantage of. Once I explained that, he was happy to comply. Now, that does not mean he leaves everything else up to me, it's just that I need him to do those two things first. The rest we can negotiate later."

When looking for chores to assign to your spouse, try these tips for gaining more acceptance and cooperation:

- Don't just tell him what to do; ask him what chores he would like to take off your hands.

- Be reasonable – the guy does work, you know. He can't be expected to come home and clean the entire house. Straightening up may be an option though.

- Find things he is good at. My husband can't clean a bathroom to save his life. He tries (oh, how he tries), but he just can't seem to get it done properly (sometimes it looks worse after he cleans it). But he is really great at doing laundry and shampooing the rugs. So guess what? He gets to do those!

On the flip side, I am absolutely lousy at taking care of the lawn and garden (I kill everything – it's a miracle my children are still alive), so he handles all outside chores while I clean the inside and keep all the closets organized.

- Find a system that works for your family. Every family – and every couple – works differently. A successful compromise for one couple may end in disaster for another. Split household chores appropriately in your house – whatever that split ends up looking like. If it works for the two of you, then go for it!

When it comes to handling those household and childcare chores, be patient and be accepting, says Connie, who has been married to Tony for 36 years. "He isn't going to do it like you would – no one can."

For instance, her husband handles the children very differently than she does. He's more of the fun guy who makes everything a game, while she is more regimented and scheduled. "The balance works well for the kids," she says.

However, problems did arise early in their parenting life when Connie expected that her husband would handle his childcare responsibilities just like she did.

"He'd rile them up right before bed and then I assumed that I was the one who had to put them to sleep, which was impossible. Finally, I handed him the baby and said, fine you energized this bunny, now you deal with it. Surprisingly, our son went right to sleep. For some reason, his father's hijinks did manage to tire him out (or maybe it was Dad's stern voice). Either way, the child went right to sleep. Just because your husband handles his fathering duties differently than a mom, doesn't mean he is doing it wrong. Give him some slack (and some credit). The dude knows what he's doing – most of the time.

No matter how quirkily your husband handles his duties, accept and appreciate them for what they are – his way. As long as things get done, who cares how different he makes the entire process?

CHAPTER SEVEN

BUILDING STRONG FAMILY TIES FOR A HAPPIER & MORE PRODUCTIVE HOMESCHOOLING EXPERIENCE

When you spend all day trying to coerce uncooperative children into getting their schoolwork done, it can sometimes be hard to remember that you are more than teacher and student – you are mother and child.

When the hassles of homeschooling and homemaking begin to take a toll on the way you look at your family, take some time to reconnect with everyone – including the kids. A good way to begin appreciating everyone again is to try some of these tips:

- Eat together as a family unit.

The results are clear: Families that eat together three to five times per week have smarter, better-behaved, more well-adjusted and outgoing kids. Their grades are better, their manners are better, and their attitudes are better. It may sound crazy to tell a homeschooling family that does virtually everything together to take some time to eat meals as a group, but the sad fact is that many homeschoolers take mealtime as free time to spend alone. Some family members eat meals at different times due to schedules or other time constraints. Even if you can't sit down and eat the main meal together several times a week (maybe dad works late), try to at least get together for dessert afterward. Breaking bread together is a very stress-free and relaxing way to hear about everyone's day and just enjoy one another's company.

- Take a few minutes each week for solo time with individual kids.

When there is so much to get done, it can be easy to forget to spend time with some of your kids – especially the quiet ones. Sarah explains how her one daughter, who is very easygoing and cooperative, went two weeks without anyone really paying any attention to her.

"The squeaky wheel definitely gets our attention around here and poor Meg just never squeaks. She takes everything in stride and does her best to get her own work done, her chores completed and so on. When I realized she hadn't handed in her history project, she burst into tears and said, 'you promised weeks ago to help me and then got busy. I asked a few times but you were so busy with the baby (who was sick) and the others. I'm sorry I didn't get it done but I needed your help!'"

How guilty can a mom feel, anyway? One way to ensure that every child gets some attention on a regular basis is to literally schedule them on your calendar. Even a 15-minute appointment every morning can give you time to touch base. This is not the only time you should spend with your child, of course, but it will ensure that no one is accidentally forgotten amidst the other chaos in your house – and life – from day to day.

- Write down five things you love about your kid each week. (Then share your list either privately or in the group.)

When Faith realized that she was always telling her kids what they did wrong – and rarely what they did right – she decided to take some time and list all of the things she absolutely loves about her kids. Once she got started, the lists grew and grew and grew. She knew it was important to share those lists with her kids – and she did.

"You can't imagine how surprised and thrilled they were to learn about all of the things that I love and appreciate about them – including some of their quirkier habits. It was such a simple way to boost their self-worth. Each says they look at themselves differently now."

Faith decided to share her observations privately for a more intimate encounter with each child, but some parents may choose to share their insights within a group setting to help others in the family appreciate their siblings' attributes more – and notice them.

- Have each member of the family share one thing another member of the family did that week that they thought was really cool, interesting, or awe-inspiring.

There are times when my children's insight, understanding, brain-power and creativity simply knock my socks off. That's when I need to take a moment and tell them so. What holds me back? Sometimes I'm just too rushed to stop what I'm doing (shame on me) and sometimes I don't want to embarrass them (phooey). Once a week, ask each person in the family to tell someone else in the family about something they did, said or tried that was really awesome in their eyes. You may be surprised at what your children observe about one another. Agnes was. She couldn't believe it when her 11-year-old said this about the 5-year-old sister he was always complaining about: "I really think it is neat how you drip your popsicles on the sidewalk on purpose so the ants get a treat too."

- Make some popcorn and snuggle up on the couch to enjoy a movie together.

Nothing can bring a family closer than sharing a bucket of popcorn and snuggling up together to laugh at a good comedy, cry at a sad drama or be thrilled by an awesome adventure!

- Have a roast for someone in the family (just be sure the person can handle it).

Now, this one can be a bit tricky. Usually it is best to make the roast recipient Mom or Dad (after all, kids love to gang up on their parents). Older children especially enjoy this fun way of bashing their parents. Just be clear on the rules and be sure to explain the difference between hurting someone's feelings and jokingly poking fun.

- Go for a family bike ride.

Biking is a fun way to get outdoors, get some exercise and spend some time together as a family. Whether you take off on a featured trail or just bike around the block, riding together is a lot of fun.

- Plan a family game night, allowing each member to choose their favorite game to play.

No matter what their age, kids love playing games. Sure, your teens may balk a bit, but trust me, almost all them end up giggling and laughing before the night is over. Just be sure to let everyone choose a game they like to ensure success for the evening. If by chance you all like the same game, have a marathon or teem up against one another.

- Go camping.

Camping isn't for everyone, but if your family likes the great outdoors, it can be a good way to escape the real world and enjoy each other in a more relaxed (and techno-free) environment. Even if you don't have the time or equipment for a real campout, try putting one together in your backyard.

- Lay out under the stars and just chat.

Remember how it used to feel to lay across the grass and stare at the stars? Have you introduced your children to this simple exercise yet? My husband and I used to do just this when we first got married. We'd lay there for hours just drinking in the night sky and chit-chatting about all sorts of things, from the mundane to the most sophisticated theological topics. Now we do the same thing with our kids. Give your children this same gift and do your own star-gazing some night.

- Share a secret.

Psst ... I bet you didn't know ... Everyone loves to be made privy to a secret, so share one with your kids. Now, it doesn't have to anything really big (and shouldn't be), but find something about yourself or someone else (within reasons) that you can share. One of my favorites was telling my 7-year-old daughter that her daddy was wearing pink underwear one day. Every time she looked at him that day she couldn't help but giggle. It was a fun way to bring us together and didn't hurt anyone by sharing this laundry secret. Use sound judgment here, and then find some things to share – secretly of course.

- Write and perform a family play for friends, neighbors and extended family.

Working on such a large-scale project can be a great way to build rapport with your kids and get to know them better as individuals. Plus it can be a lot of fun! When Carol did this with her family she learned that her daughter was a real drama queen, her son had a talent for sound and lighting, and her smallest son actually was very good at creating beautiful sets. Without this project she may have never discovered her children's hidden talents.

- Build a snowman together.

How fun is that? What more is there to say?

- Play hooky together for just one day.

Remember the thrill of ditching school for the day? About twice a year my mother would get us up, get us dressed for school, grab our backpacks, and put us in the car, only we never made it to school, we played hooky for the day. It was always an exciting adventure! Just because you are homeschooling doesn't mean you can't do the same. Pick a day (and day) and change up the schedule, or simply blow off your classes.

- Say thank you for something someone did for you this week.

In the midst of the daily chaos it can be difficult to always find the time to say thank you for a job well done. My 13-year-old is quick to remind me that I never say thank you when she takes the lead and helps her brother or cleans up without being asked, and you know what? She's right. Sit down each week and find one thing to thank each member of your family for. You know what my son said the first week we tried this experiment? "Thanks mom for teaching me multiplication, even though I hate it." Now that's gratitude!

- Acknowledge a job well done.

Some weeks are harder than most, but let's face it, no one can go an entire week without doing something right. Be sure to take the time and tell your kids and your spouse what they did right this week. You'll be surprised at how much their attitudes and behavior will improve.

- Attend religious services and activities together.

One of the best ways to grow as a family is to spend time worshiping our Lord together. Joining a church family and participating in a variety of religious activities is a wonderful way to teach your children about what you believe, the relationships you cherish, and your true morals. Guiding our children down the right path isn't always easy. Being able to share that journey with a group of like-minded Christians can not only help you get through the homeschool years, but also can help your family get closer as they discover the truth of God's love together.

Sunday School and church services are important, but so is participating in other groups, such as the church softball team, Boys Brigade, transportation ministry, homeless ministries, and so on. By working side by side with your children you can learn about the others' strengths (and weaknesses) and begin to appreciate the wonderful gifts each member of your family has. Plus, working in ministry together can help to open your children's eyes to the way others live and work in the world.

When Kathy first started taking her children on runs for Meals on Wheels, she thought it was a good way to help them learn to interact with people of all ages while providing an important service. Little did she realize the impact those short visits would have on their clients, as well as her children. Today, her oldest (now 24) works with senior citizens on the mission field full time and her 19-year-old is showing a passion for working in geriatric healthcare care. "It was while delivering meals to our neighbors that they began to see the privilege of caring for all of God's people, no matter what their age or circumstances," Kathy says.

When it comes to building a more harmonious home and school environment, most veteran homeschoolers agree on one thing: it's a team effort. Families that do not learn how to work as a team will fail. Homeschooling isn't just a commitment to your children's education – it is a lifestyle. Unless everyone is on board and willing to work together, you will experience more chaos than calm. But work to build a stronger family unit (and marriage), and that team will begin to run more smoothly (and quietly).

Of course, this can take some innovative action and energy, but imagine how much more smoothly your days will run when everyone feels appreciated and loved. The bickering will lessen (I'm certainly not going to say it will go away), and everyone's attitude will be adjusted.

Whew! A harmonious home is achievable – if you are all willing to begin working more as a team rather than as independents living, working and schooling under the same roof.

PENCIL TIP

Teach Your Children About Life

One of the biggest benefits of handling your children's education at home is that it affords you the time to teach some of the most important life lessons they will need to succeed in the future. For many homeschooling families that means integrating home courses, gardening, finance, and so much more, into their curriculum. While these are important subjects to tack on to your school schedule, also consider that you're teaching your children about home, life and marriage. When children are taught about home finances, they are less likely to grumble when you say no to the $80 sneakers "everyone else is wearing." Oftentimes they will even take it upon themselves to look for sales and bargains for specialty items they want and need. Planting a garden together not only offers some great educational opportunities, but also gives you all the chance to work as a family team. Combining home and school activities is a fantastic way to build bonds between siblings and create lasting relationships between children and their parents.

CHAPTER EIGHT

TAKING TIME FOR YOURSELF- HOW TO RECHARGE AND REJUVENATE

" You're wound tighter than a ball of rubber bands. It is time you stopped and did something for yourself!"

His words hit me as hard as if he had slapped me across the face. Oh, how I wanted to stop running on the constant treadmill of life, but I couldn't! There was too much to do and if I stopped – for even a moment – I felt as if my whole world would fly out of control. Little did I realize that it already had.

If there is one thing I am horrible at it is juggling too many things at once. I often have balls flying off in all directions. For some, that isn't a real problem. They simply pick up the balls they have dropped and keep moving forward. Not me. I take one dropped ball as a sign of complete failure. I become extremely overwhelmed, anxious, and well, just plain crabby. (There's another word for it, but I chose not to use that one here.)

Unable to acknowledge the fact that I need to stop and rest, it has always been up to my husband to slap me back into reality – not literally of course! "Say no ... slow down ... cut things out ... forget trying to be perfect ... let the house go ...take a break ..." these are all things he has told me over the years, only I rarely listen. After all, who is he to tell me to slow down? Doesn't he know that if I don't do it, no one will?

Eventually I crack into a jumble of tears and exhaustion and either end up sick for a few days, in which case nature makes me take a much-needed break, or I become so exhausted that I can't accomplish much anyway, and need to take a rest from it all.

The problem with the way I handle the overwhelming stresses of life, family, work, home and now homeschool, is that it literally sucks the joy from my days. His way would be so much better.

"Go out with your friends for a while. Go downstairs and scrapbook if you like. Go shopping." Now who else's husband tells them to do that? If only I would heed his advice once in a while, I would be so much happier and content. But wait! It's time to pick up our daughter from her job at the library ...

OK, I'm back and none too soon. It's almost time to make dinner before I clean up and then head back to the office to try and finish this project (which by the way is four days away from deadline – yikes!). See what I mean? It's too much stuff to cram into a single day. So what is the answer?

First and foremost, my husband claims it is to acknowledge that I'm a part of this family too – and I deserve a break. Wow, what a concept! I want to hear more. How about you?

One of the hardest things for any mother to admit is that yes, I can take some time out for myself. I am worth it! Our lives revolve so much around our kids, our husbands, our homes – and when we homeschool, our children's education – that it simply does not leave much (if any) time for ourselves. So we go through our days taking care of everyone else's needs and neglecting our own. There simply is no time leftover for ourselvesus. No matter how much it is needed (or wanted), we simply can't take a time out to enjoy ourselves – or can we?

The problem, I have learned, is that failing to take care of ourselves can result in a lot of other problems, including illness, stress, depression, anxiety and Crabby Mom Syndrome, just to name a few. Divorce, too, can be a nasty side effect of an unhappy, unfulfilled and exhausted mom. Besides, how can you be an effective teacher if you resent the time spent trying to teach your kids all of the lessons of life – including school-related ones?

Hey mom, you've got a lot on your plate (I know), but you have got to take some time out for yourself! How, you may ask, can you manage to find even a few moments for yourself? Begin with these ideas:

1. Get control of the schedule.

We talked about scheduling our days earlier in the book, but what if you simply can't find any time left over for yourself? Drastic times require drastic measures: start slashing *other* people's activities.

Honestly now, do each of your children need to participate in a club, sport and music lesson every week? One mom I know decided to cut her kids music lessons to every other week and suddenly added three hours of time to her schedule for herself! Another mom opted for allowing her children to join only a scout troop that met every other week instead of every week and gained an extra four hours per month!

Then there's Lori, who has a whopping seven kids! Until recently, each of her kids was involved in three to five extracurricular activities each week. Not only did Lori need to factor in the time the activity took, but also travel time. She felt as if she was always dropping someone off somewhere or picking someone up. That's when she decided to take drastic measures: she cut everyone off cold turkey. Now that was brave.

Lori began her experiment on the first day of summer. She figured summer was a better time to cut out activities since school was not in session and the kids had more free time anyway.

At first, they balked. Then they complained. Then they whined. And then a miracle happened: they began to find other ways to fill their time. With no TV in their home (yes, this mom is really brave), those darned kids started reading more, playing games together, inviting friends to swim in their pool, construct a playhouse in the backyard, and more. Her 10-year-old began building model rockets and her 5-year-old took up crocheting, thanks to a big sister who showed her how.

When summer ended, she asked each child what activities they missed the most. Two kids said their sports teams, one said her music lessons, three others insisted they wanted to go back to scouts and 4H and the last one said, "Nothing really." Whew!

"And to think I wasted all of that time, energy and gas schlepping to activities and clubs that my kids didn't even care that much about," she laments. Today, each child is allowed to pick two activities that they really like and she makes sure they get there. Right now only four out of the seven kids are in two activities; the rest chose only one – their absolute favorite. It seems they enjoy having more relaxed time at home (and out of the car) too!

As for Lori, she is now involved in two of her own activities, taking a much-needed exercise break every evening and a photography class once a month. All that extra free time is devoted to spending quality time together as a family.

"It has really been a blessing to slash our schedule," she says. "We rarely even need to consult a calendar anymore. Everyone knows what they have going on and where they need to be and when, and that's it. No more running around like maniacs. Life is busy enough with seven kids, there is no need to add to our aggravation."

We could all take a lesson from Lori. Most of us have schedules that are so jam-packed with activities that we have not even taken the chance to figure out if we like them or not. We think that just because an opportunity becomes available to our children they must be involved in it. The fact is, they don't. Teaching our children how to pace their days and their lives is just as important as involving them in all sorts of activities that may only serve to exhaust and frustrate them. Choose what they are most passionate about and let the rest go.

For Karen, trimming her schedule was more about her own need to comply with others' expectations than to involve her children in stuff.

"I just can't say no when someone asks me to do something" she admits. "I feel so guilty – especially if no one else volunteers to do it – that I just tack one more thing on to my to-do list until I am so overwhelmed that I end up getting mad at everyone and doing a lousy job all around."

Karen's answer: she has found a friend who says no for her. "She acts like my personal assistant. When I am asked to do something at church or co-op or even the neighborhood I say, 'Oh, I first must check with Carol. She's in charge of my schedule, you know.' At first people thought I was crazy, but now they just accept that Carol is my scheduling person and sometimes they simply ask her first if I have time for something, which is a real hoot considering she is just a friend I use to help me stick to my ultimate plan – to have more time for myself."

When it comes to your daily, weekly and monthly schedules, take some time to revaluate all items listed to see what can go. If you can't bring yourself to stop doing as much on a permanent basis, at least try Lori's approach: tell everyone that you need a three-month break from outside activities and volunteer efforts to get your house in order. Who can argue your need to take care of your home and family? Once you take a break you may be surprised at what few things you really want to add back to your schedule.

Faye was surprised that once she took a break, her mind was much clearer on the things she wanted o do. "I really missed helping out in the nursery at church. I did not miss helping out with the annual block party in our neighborhood. Now I am only involved in the things I enjoy and say no to the rest. The biggest benefit (besides more time for myself) is that I now have spare time to say yes to really great opportunities that arise at the spur of the moment. In the past I would miss out on fun and productive projects simply because something else was taking up my time."

2. De-clutter your home and classroom.

While we are on the topic of trimming your schedule of activities, let's discuss de-cluttering your home, office and homeschool classroom. Teachers are notorious for saving every scrap of paper around, and so are moms. Now is not the time to be nostalgic or to worry about what supplies you may need in two or three years. Just because you "may" use it in the future does not mean you have to keep it. The odds are good all of those cans and bottles that you are saving in the basement will never be put to use, so ditch them now.

The less stuff you have cluttering your home, the less you will have to clean up (and around). Be notorious when it comes to de-cluttering your home. Get rid of everything you have not put to good use in at least a year. Save only the most precious mementos and trash the rest. I give each child one file box per year to save special school items and projects. Once that box is full, that's it. If they want to save something else they have to get rid of another item. Not only am I keeping my home better organized, but I am also teaching my children some important life lessons.

When it comes to school supplies, Meghan has adopted a very useful strategy. "I used to hit the before-school super sales every year and stock up on so many supplies that they usually got broken, trashed or misplaced, wasting space, time and money. I still go to those sales, but I limit my purchases to only those items I know we will use. Just because crayons are a quarter a box does not mean we need 20 boxes to get through the year. I usually buy enough items for each child to begin the school year and a duplicate set to replace lost items mid-year. Then I assemble my own emergency box full of extra tape, glue sticks, pencils, erasers, tablets, etc. That's it.

Each child gets a fully stocked pencil box in September and another in February."

So far her plan has worked well. Once the children realized that they could not just go to the cabinet and grab another pencil they were much more diligent about putting their things away.

April uses another strategy for weaning out excess school supplies: money. "Twice a year I go through my curriculum, manipulatives and other teaching supplies and decide what we are finished with, what we will never use and what we hated the first time around. Then I sell those things to other homeschoolers. We put that money in a special jar for other supplies we may need and special field trips. One a year we made enough to take all four children for a weekend getaway to Washington, D.C., just from getting rid of stuff that was cluttering my school cabinets."

Handling the chaos of clutter can be a torturous affair for many moms. It takes time, effort and emotion to sift through your children's old books, toys, curriculum and other belongings to get rid of them. I take a completely different approach: I switch houses with a friend. Since it is always easier to throw out other people's stuff, my best friend and I de-clutter each other's homes. Since we are such good friends, we have a real grasp on what the other really wants – and needs – to keep, so I feel pretty safe allowing her free reign of my closets. The only problem is, sometimes (especially when it comes to curriculum) I want to bring home her leftovers. Allowing my friend to decide what we have outgrown has freed me from the decision-making required to clean up our chaos, and that has saved us hours of wasted time.

Not ready to allow someone else to de-clutter your home and decide which belongings stay and which can go? Then take a tip from the pros:

Tip #1:

Take 15 minutes twice a day and work as fast as you can to simply fill up garbage bags. At least this way you begin to weed out the garbage.

Tip #2:

If you are unsure about keeping an item, put it in a sealed bag (and date it), then set it in the basement for one month. At the end of the month throw out any bags that remain unopened – don't open them now! The odds are you will not even remember what was in it in the first place.

Tip #3:

If you have not used it, looked at it, worn it or thought about it in six to 12 months, then get rid of it – now!

Tip #4:

Never bring any new item into your home without throwing out another item you no longer need or use. This will help to keep your clutter under control.

Tip #5:

Feeling guilty about getting rid of your children's special projects? Take pictures of them and then display those pictures, that way everyone can enjoy the memories!

Tip #6:

Stop wasting time sifting through those junk drawers for special treasures you "have to save." Close your eyes and dump the drawer in the closest garbage can – it only takes about five seconds. Remember, it's called a "junk drawer" for a reason.

3. Start delegating.

You might think that you have to do it all yourself, but you don't. Nothing is more overwhelming than trying to do it all on your own. From your youngest to your oldest, begin dividing chores and household responsibilities between members of the clan. Even some schoolwork can be delegated. Let older students mentor younger ones. That provides some important lessons in life. Small children can pick up their toys, wipe down the table, put away silverware, and even take out the trash. Older children can take partial or full responsibility for changing the linens, cleaning out the refrigerator, washing the dishes, cooking meals and even caring for younger siblings.

4. Get rid of the busywork.

Too many homeschooling moms add more busywork to their days (and their students' days) than is necessary. Does you child really need to practice their handwriting every day? Maybe. Maybe not. If the answer is not, then cut it from your school schedule. Don't just add a subject or a project because you think you should – or worse yet, because everyone else is doing it. Concentrate on the subjects and topics you know your child needs most –

and is most interested in – and forget the rest. There's nothing worthy of wasting your time. Cut out the extra and you will all enjoy the work you *do* study. You might even find that your school day is a bit shorter when you get rid of all that nonessential busywork.

5. Learn to say no to others.

Now Mom, I know that it is a hard word to say, but let's practice. *N-O! No ... No ... No!* See that wasn't so hard, was it? So why is it that we find that simple two-letter word so difficult to spit out when someone asks us to help out with vacation Bible school, teaching a co-op class, babysitting a neighbor's child, or even taking on an extra shift at work? *No* used to be an easy word to say. After all, it was part of our daily mantra when our children were toddlers. "No, don't touch that!" "No, you can not eat cookies dipped in orange juice for breakfast!" "No, we can't watch TV all day." *No ... no ... no ... no.*

I have a theory that we say *no* so much as we were trying to keep our active toddlers safe that we actually no ourselves out. By the time our children reach school age, we have forgotten how to say it or are just plain sick of saying the word – to anyone. So we don't, and we manage to get ourselves into a lot of time-wasting jams. By learning to discern what we have the time, interest and energy to handle – and saying no to the rest – we can more easily find the time to lift many of the burdens that are overwhelming our daily lives, as well as our homeschools.

Here's another tip: learn to say *no* to your children when they want to get involved in yet another activity. I have a hard time with this one. I like homeschooling because it gives us the time to devote to our children's special interests. Unfortunately, those interests tend to get expanded when you have more time, which can make it difficult to say no when a unique opportunity arises.

My daughter is very involved in community theater, which is wonderful. But we are learning how to balance a hectic rehearsal schedule and other fun teen stuff. It took our first year of theater involvement to understand just how time-consuming it could be and to realize that if she wanted to audition for one show after another, she would have to trim some other activities from her social schedule. That was a hard lesson for both of us – after all, who wants to give up anything? But, after trekking from activity to activity for months, I was beat and she was beginning to think the world revolved around her and her social calendar; two things that needed to be dealt with. Now she is allowed to be in a show only if she gives up her other extracurricular activities during the most stringent part of the rehearsal schedule. If she is not willing to do that, than she is not permitted to participate.

As a mom, it can be difficult to look at that sweet face and say *no*, but it is our duty to do it – for ourselves and our kids! They do not have to be involved in everything that becomes available. Actually, it is better if they are not. Learning how to pick and choose what is best for us is an important skill for a happier, more blissful – and less stressful – future.

6. Learn to say yes to yourself.

While you are saying *no* to your children, learn to say *yes* to yourself. How many times have you put off doing something you would really like to do because it conflicted with your child's wants and schedule? Mom, here is a bit of advice: knock it off! It is OK to think of yourself once in a while. You deserve a break and you deserve some fun too! Yes, you are a member of this family and you have a right to concentrate on your own wants and needs once in a while. Too many moms go for months (or even years) without ever taking a breath or a time-out just for themselves. This leads to frustration, stress, illness and feelings of resentment. If you do not take care of yourself, your entire body will begin to show the signs – you'll gain weight, you'll get wrinkled, you'll be crabby all of the time, and you may even come down with a disease. Put bluntly, you'll get old faster than you should.

My husband put it to me this way: "If you run yourself into the ground, these kids are going to have to go back to school. I can't teach them and go to work full time." That threat was enough to get me to take some time for myself.

Want to know the real secrets to a more youthful you? Take time out for you. Pamper yourself. Relax. Enjoy life again. Your house will not fall apart. Your children will suddenly not become stupid, and the state will not come in a take your kids to real school because you are failing their education. You deserve a break, so take it!

Once you have cleared out your schedule, cleared out your home, and opened up some free time, you will be better able to concentrate on yourself – without the guilt.

Now, what should you do to take better care of yourself? Let's look at some ways you can pamper yourself and give yourself the respite you need to be a better mother, a better wife, and a better teacher.

Start exercising.

You have to be kidding right? This chapter was supposed to be about nurturing my own inner (and outer) self – putting the joy back into my life, and my editor wants me to include a section on the importance of exercise? She's got to be kidding!

That was my first response when seeing all of the topics I needed to include in this book. Exercise? Bah, Humbug! Once I calmed down, I started to think about it. OK, so finding time to exercise isn't really a priority for most of us and for good reason – there are not enough hours in the day for all the stuff that has to get done, so who can squeak out 45 minutes every morning to do something you don't really want to do anyway?

But think about it. Exercising isn't just about losing weight or even staying healthy. It is also a good way to increase circulation, boost your metabolism and get your energy back. These are all things you need in order to get through the rigors of a typical school day. Exercise can help you to boost your levels of concentration and relieve stress. Plus, if you choose the right activity, it can be a lot of fun.

Now, consider the impact of exercise on your kids. If they see you indulging in a physical activity, the odds are they will do it too. That will help them to increase their own concentration, stay fit, be healthier, stay calmer during the school day and have some fun with you. Plus, you can clock the time they spend exercising as Phys Ed in their portfolio.

Teaching your kids the benefits of a regular exercise routine is important to ensure that they don't fall victim to obesity or other health issues. Staying active throughout your lifetime is vital to living longer, so why not start now? Choose an activity that you can all enjoy (basketball, swimming, hiking, bicycling, etc.), and begin a daily exercise regimen. You will be amazed at how it improves your school day, not to mention the way you all feel.

Some families prefer to start their school day with a quick walk or game, while others use the promise of some physical activity at the end of the day to get through their class work. Still others pencil in a special recess time midway through the day to help everyone refocus on the task at hand.

If you are a mom who needs some time to exercise alone, take it. I walk the dog twice a day, plus I ride a stationery bike while my children work on their spelling lists and reading assignments. If they get stuck, they can come to me for help, but otherwise I have at least a half an hour free to get in a little workout.

Eat right.

How can eating right make your turn a chaotic homeschool into a calmer one? Consider the impact a poor diet can have on everyone in your home and school:

- **A lack of concentration** – Without the right mix of proteins and essential fatty acids (EFAs), concentration levels will suffer. In one important study it was noted that teenage boys who were given Omega-3 and Omega-6 supplements tested much higher on standardized tests than their classmates who were not given the supplements. Eating more fresh fruits and vegetables, fish and other EFAs can help boost your children's ability to retain knowledge, thus creating a more educationally rich environment in your homeschool.

- **Jitteriness** – Too much sugar, caffeine and dyes an all affect a child's ability to sit still and work on their studies. Eating a more nutrient-rich diet can help both teacher and student to get down to work.

- **Stress** – A poor diet can cause your entire body to feel stressed, which can make it more difficult to handle the daily tasks at hand. Providing your body's organs and cells with the right vitamins, minerals and supplements can help to reduce your overall stress levels and get you through those hectic home and school days with ease.

- **Poor health** – Poor eating habits often result in more colds, flus and other health related issues – for everyone in the family. Eat right and avoid the hectic days of trying to care for sick ones and well ones, and keeping up with schoolwork and housework – all while you are not feeling well either.

- **Sluggishness** – You need a certain amount of fats and protein to produce the energy your body needs to get through a typical day – especially one that involves handling your children's education, as well as your home and family (plus work).

- **Allergies** – The affects of allergies can have a dramatic impact on your children's ability to get their schoolwork done. Even something as simple as hay fever can keep them feeling irritable, uncooperative and lethargic. Who can learn anything when they feel awful? From food allergies to other reactions, your diet can have a big impact on how you feel and how your body reacts to the things in its environment. Give your body healthy immune-boosting foods and you can fight all sorts of ailments, including allergies.

•

Nurture your relationships. (ALL OF THEM)

Homeschooling can seem very isolating at times. No matter how hard you try to socialize your kids, you may be stuck feeling like you are all alone in your commitment to provide the best learning environment for your children. That's why it is so imperative that you nurture the relationships in your life. Don't allow yourself to become isolated in a world of children and schoolbooks. Get out and foster some adult time with those people you enjoy spending time with.

Keep in touch with your extended friends and family.

Keeping in touch with faraway friends and relatives isn't always easy when your days are full. Add to that the aspect of negativity that some people may have about your choice to homeschool, and you could be left feeling as if all of your friends are off enjoying life while you are bound at home. First, figure out who is only going to make you feel bad about this important life choice and limit your interaction with them (for now, at least). Next, pick a few people in your inner circle that you would love to reconnect – or stay connected – with. Then make it a point to interact with them on a regular basis by:

- **Phoning** – There are just some people you need to talk to from time to time. If there is someone in your life (albeit your mother, a close friend, or even a close neighbor that you enjoy chatting with), make a point to pick up the phone and call from time to time. For Sandra, the best way to keep in touch with her mom was to schedule an appointment. "I call her every Monday at 10 a.m. while the kids are taking an online health class. That's the only 45 minutes in a week that I can guarantee I'll be free. While

I may sneak in other phone calls during the week, we both count on that special time to reconnect."

- **Drop in for a visit** – There's nothing like a quick cup of tea with a close friend when your day seems out of control. If you have a close friend who's also a neighbor, don't be shy – drop in for a quick chat or that cup of tea. Oftentimes it is this type of impromptu visit that best settles the chaos. Of course, be careful not to infringe on your friend's time. But if you are close, you'll know when it's OK and when it is not.

- **Email or Facebook** – Sometimes the only time to chat is late at night or early in the morning. That's when email comes in handy. You can each respond at your own convenience. For those who Facebook or use some other type of social network, getting together with old or long-distance friends is easier than ever these days.

- **Send a note or letter** – It may seem archaic, but when all else fails, you can always keep in touch with a good old-fashioned letter. So uncommon these days, a personal note can often connect you even more with those you want to keep in touch with.

- **Plan a visit** – One of the best ways to stay in touch with friends and family members is to plan a formal visit or party. When Andrea realized that she hadn't seen or spoken with her best friend from childhood in almost five years, she called her up and planned a get together. "It was so wonderful to see her again. We connected right away; as if we had never been apart. We now get together once a year, alternating who makes the five-hour drive. When our children were very young, we split the drive, meeting at a really neat amusement center halfway between our two hometowns. Our friendship is priceless, so it is worth this minimal effort once a year to keep in touch."

Patty too, loves to stay in touch with the many people who come in and out of her life, so she opts to throw an open house picnic every summer at her home. Inviting all sorts of people she would otherwise rarely see (aunts, cousins, work acquaintances, school parents, etc.), her family welcomes just about everyone in their life to their home every July for an old-fashioned picnic full of games, water fun, food and fellowship. "It's been a great way to connect and we never really know who will show up from year to year. One summer we only had 10 guests making the party very intimate; then the next year almost 80 people showed up. It is exciting to see what sort of gathering we'll have from summer to summer."

While taking time out for the people in your life is important, too many homeschool moms forget to nurture the most important relationship they have – with God.

"Prayer was the last thing on my list," admits Beth shyly. "I yearned to have a more intimate relationship with God, but simply could not find the time to open my Bible and pray any meaningful prayers. Then one day I decided I was just going to pray quick one-liners every time a thought came into my head and you know what? Before lunchtime I had actually had a meaningful conversation with God. It wasn't hard and it didn't take a lot of time, but it was real. I learned an important lesson that day: you don't have to be in a pew or even on your knees to connect with our Lord. You just have to be open to his voice – and His help.

I'll admit that I don't always find the time to sit down and have a "real" devotion, but I can honestly say that not a day goes by when God and I don't chat while I'm doing dishes or walking the dog or even standing over my reluctant reader. Once I turned to God in prayer with all my angst and frustration, our homeschool days got a lot easier. So, my advice to any harried homeschool mom is to get reconnected with God. You may just be surprised at how much better everything else in your life – and homeschool – falls into place.

- **Put romance back in your marriage.**

As we've discussed in length, creating a happy home and homeschool requires having happy parents. Nothing can make your relationship stronger than adding a spark of romance to your days. Don't neglect the most important relationship in your life – your marriage. Do whatever is necessary to make each other feel wanted, loved and cared for.

Send him romantic message at work, bring her home flowers, cook his favorite meal (you know, the one you hate), watch a chick flick with her (and stay awake). Being romantic doesn't have to be all about hearts and flowers, but it must come from the heart. Some of the most romantic things women have reported over the years have been acts of pure kindness from their spouses, like: taking the lead and putting the kids to bed without being asked; bringing home her favorite chocolate cake from the bakery for no reason (or better yet ,bringing home just one cupcake – for her – so she can indulge in something that is truly just hers); giving her a foot massage; snuggling on the couch while watching TV; holding hands in public; and believe it or not, cleaning the house and even washing the car. It seems that women view romance a bit differently from men and that's OK. While no woman will turn down flowers and diamonds, just being appreciated and pampered for 20 minutes is often enough.

- **Find a friend.**

There is nothing like having a good girlfriend to cry with, laugh with, complain to and just vent with. If it weren't for my best friend, I think I would have exploded years ago. There have been times in my life when I was girlfriend-less due to heavy work schedules, a lack of social interaction, and even my own failure to reach out and find someone to call friend. Those were the darkest and loneliest times of my life. Now, let me explain.

I consider my husband my very best friend in all thethe entire world, but sometimes you just need another girl to talk to. Who else understands PMS, sore nursing breasts, a procrastinating husband and a cranky 12-year-old? A best friend can make you laugh at the stupid things you are taking way too seriously (without eliciting a fight – or tears – like your husband can) and she can bluntly tell you that *Yes dear, those pants do make your butt look big,* without you throwing a trauma and saying how she doesn't love you (or your butt) anymore. Better yet, it is only a BFF who can get away with taking you out for a hot fudge sundae after the trials and tears of bathing suit shopping.

So dear burned-out mom, find yourself a friend. She may just be the perfect person to help you put your day in perspective.

- **Find a prayer partner.**

When our pastor suggested that we all find a prayer partner for the coming year (it was December), my first thought was, "Yeah right. Like I have time to meet with someone every week and pray for an hour together."

Unsure about this new role, but unwilling to be the only deadbeat who didn't take a prayer partner card when leaving the sanctuary that Sunday, I agreed to give it a try. I sure am glad I did. I was assigned Stella, a lovely 78-year-old woman who has raised 12 children of her own while still working as a seamstress out of her home after her husband was killed in a farming accident. I had talked with Stella briefly over the years, but never really had the chance to get to know her. I soon found out all that this spunky almost-80-something had to offer.

We decided to meet for breakfast one Saturday morning when my husband was home to set the ground rules for this new endeavor. The first thing she said was, "Honey, I know how busy you are and you don't have time to sit with me every week, so let's do this: You call or email me when you need some prayer and I'll get on it. If you think of something we can both be praying about (world affairs, a sick person at church, etc.), drop me an email. My great-grandson hooked me up with this Internet thing and I kind of like it. When you have time to get together, we will. But right now, your kids and school come first. Let me pick you up in prayer and we'll just see how that goes."

Wow, I had really lucked out! I was going to get to do what the pastor asked and not really have to do anything. Before long, Stella was emailing me the most beautiful prayers for me and my family. I was awestruck and inspired to do the same for her. I began praying whenever I had a spare moment for this dear little lady. Then we started chatting on the phone. As I opened up to her about my frustrations at home (and school) and my guilt for not having enough time or energy for it all, she began praying for God to give me more discernment for the things I tackle, more energy, and more love. And those things came.

Soon, Stella and I were chatting every day on the phone (some of my favorite times of the day). Then my kids and I started dropping in to see her. It was my daughter who began to see things around her house that needed fixing, cleaning or just handled, so we'd make surprise work trips to get some stuff done.

By the end of the first year, Stella and I had become great friends. I have learned so much from her about handling a family, household chores and husbands, as well as how to appreciate the days we are in and letting go of the things that are blocking us from really embracing the life we are given.

My kids have been blessed too, with a grandmother-type who lives just a mile or so down the road, and the opportunity to give back to her in tangible ways – to show her how much she means to us. Finding a prayer partner to keep you on track spiritually and to share your thoughts, dreams and frustrations with can be a wonderful way to forge new friendships. Step up your spiritual journey and of course, get some prayerful help when you need it!

- **Find some support.**

Homeschooling can be rough. No matter how good you are at it. How organized your schedule and how disciplined your children, there will still be days when you feel like throwing in the towel and putting your kids on that big yellow bus – no matter where it's going.

That's when you need someone to help you remember why you homeschool and maybe even to help you figure out how to move past certain growing pains in the classroom. Homeschool support groups come in all shapes and sizes. Some consist of three or four families, some hundreds. Some meet on a regular basis, while others meet on an as-needed one. Some offer speakers and workshops, others offer only social activities. Some invite kids along, others are for parents only. Some meet in person, others online. No matter where you live and what your interests, there is a homeschool support group out there for you. All you have to do is figure out what you want and need from this type of group and look for it.

Not sure where to look for a homeschool support group? Check with your local church.

With more than 50 percent of all homeschool families considering themselves conservative Christians, the local church seems to the best place to connect. Housing support groups. co-ops and even curriculum fairs, the local church strives to provide the help and support Christian homeschoolers need. Sure, there are a lot of secular groups out there, but finding one that strives to help Christian parents break secular roles and offer a more meaningful spiritual base to their school environment and curriculum choices can help to validate your reasons for homeschooling in the first place, while offering important guidance along the way that you just can't get from outside sources.

- **Pamper yourself.**

While a trip to the spa may be nice, pampering yourself doesn't have to require a big investment of your time or money. I will never forget the episode of "The Middle," a family-related comedy, when a co-worker talks a harried working mother into taking just 15 minutes to herself. She snuck into the cruddy bathroom of the car dealership she worked for and turned off her cell phone. Then she painted her toenails; jumped through the fresh scent of air freshener and relaxed her tired eyes by laying maxi pads across them. She finished her time by reading a complete magazine article – the whole thing! She emerged from that dirty bathroom feeling refreshed and ready to tackle what lay ahead in her day. I laughed until my side ached. My husband didn't get it. He thought the whole scene was stupid. I knew better – it was life as a mom.

When that sort of 15-minute spa treatment looks really inviting (and works), you know that it is time to pamper yourself. Instead of retreating into a dirty restroom and covering your eyes with maxi pads, try indulging in a bubble bath before bed; buy yourself some fresh flowers at the grocery store; purchase some new perfume; or one of my favorites – buy some new fluffy white socks. I just love fluffy white socks in the wintertime! Make a cup of hot cocoa and call your mom to make you some homemade brownies. You will be amazed at what some of these very simple things can do to brighten your day and your mood.

Find 15 minutes every morning to jump-start your day.

Taking just 15 minutes in the morning to focus on yourself and your day can make everything that happens thereafter a bit more bearable. Wake up with your favorite cup of coffee or tea. Read a chapter in that novel you have wanted to get to. Sit on your back porch or deck and drink in the morning air. Read a single Bible verse or passage. Pray.

Just a few minutes each morning for yourself and to connect with God in order to see His plan for your day can help to better focus your efforts in the direction they are meant to go, and can give you a much better outlook on your day by helping to calm your senses and awaken your inner spirit.

End your day on a calmer quieter note.

A relatively easy way to give yourself the attention you need and deserve is to find a way to calmly end your day. Here are some suggestions other moms use:

* Take 10 minutes to pray.

* Read a magazine article or book

chapter just for fun (no educational materials allowed!).

* Take a warm shower.

* Curl up with a hot drink.

* Put on your most comfy jammies.

* Watch a TV program or movie that only you like.

* Listen to some music.

* Go to sleep to the sounds of nature.

Reconnect with your spiritual self.

For many homeschooling families, a flourishing spiritual life is very important. Yet, those same moms who take great pains to increase their children's spiritual awareness often allow their own spiritual life to wane due to the other tasks in their life. Some ways in which you can nurture your own religious beliefs and spiritual life include:

- taking time out each day to read your Bible

- joining a woman's Bible study (some churches even offer babysitting during daytime classes)

- going on a spiritual retreat (either alone or with a friend or loved one)

- praying

- reading a two- to five-minute devotional each day

- starting a journal listing your thoughts, dreams, spiritual ravings and prayers. Be sure to include both praises and requests.

- finding a prayer partner – this will force you to stay connected spiritually

Breathe ...

Can you believe that less than half the population breathes correctly? For something we all do every minute of every day, it is hard to believe that so many of us are doing it inefficiently. Most people fail to breathe deeply enough to actually fill their lungs completely with oxygen, thus depriving their mind and body of the oxygen it needs to feel its best.

In an attempt to look thinner, most people suck in their belly while they breathe, but nature actually requires you to breathe with your belly puffed out. Think I'm crazy? Watch a newborn baby breathe. What does their belly do? It puffs out as they inhale and pulls in with their exhale. This is how they bring in enough oxygen to their lungs and body. Try it. You will be amazed at how much fuller your lungs become.

So what can this do to make your homeschool chaos calm? While better breathing may not help the harried pace of the day go away, taking in more oxygen can have a calming effect of both mind and body. Plus, it can give you more energy to tackle the tasks at hand.

When life begins to get to hard to handle, take a few minutes to breathe deeply and watch how your stress seems to melt away.

Meditation and yoga are two other effective ways to calm your anxieties and give your day a more peaceful feel. While meditation offers the opportunity to clear your mind and focus your energies on the day ahead, yoga uses a combination of stretching poses aimed at releasing the body's energies and breathing techniques to calm and focus yourself. Both require a little guidance, so sign up for a class or buy a good DVD to show you the proper methods of both meditation and yoga for best results.

Self-care is an important aspect of homeschooling. Why? Because a mom who does not take the time to take care of her own physical, emotional and spiritual needs will not be able to take care of all of her family's needs for an extended period of time.

Homeschooling can sap your energy in no time. Without a plan to help curb the things that are overwhelming you, you will be unable to cope with even the most menial troubles, let alone take care of everyone else's needs – and teach too! Taking time out to take care of your health and well-being is a vital component to running a homeschool that is both effective and fun! After all, you brought your kids home to learn for a reasons – because you can teach them best. So give them your best, and nothing less! That requires being at your best and you can't be your best if you never take time out to nurture yourself.

Some homeschooling moms don't take daily or weekly time, but instead plan whole weekends (or even weeks) away from the humdrum daily activities of home and school. This can be refreshing for the entire family since the kids get to stay with Dad, Grandma or friends during your absence and you get to, well, be free.

Beth, a homeschool mom of four, admits that she whisks away with her husband for a long weekend every fall and spring and loves it. This is time for them to just spend together. Their only rule: no one can talk about the house, the kids or school! That may sound wonderful, but consider this drawback: "The first time we tried this we didn't speak the entire weekend," Beth admits. "That's when it dawned on us that we had forgotten how to be 'us' and just enjoy each other. That was a big eye-opener for us. Our marriage has improved dramatically since we started getting away to just be a couple again. Luckily we have a great support system who can care for our children while we get away, but even if we didn't, we would find some way to sneak off for a few hours once in a while to reconnect."

Amy, on the other hand, admits that she needs girl time with her own set of BFFs. "There's nothing quite like staying up all night eating all the stuff you won't let your kids eat, watching chick flicks, crying and laughing together and even playing a round or two of truth or dare. It's like being in college again and I can't get enough!" That's why Amy schedules one weekend a year away with a group of close girlfriends.

Then there is Debra, who likes the quiet of being alone. With no family living within a three-hour's drive, she can feel a bit overwhelmed at times with the responsibilities of home, family and schoolwork. With no time for herself (I don't even bother closing the bathroom door anymore, she confesses, since there is always someone knocking on it anyway), Debra says she needs to just be alone sometimes. Taking a cue from her, her husband Alan has started making the trek with the kids to his mother's twice a year for a weekend visit – minus mom.

"It's heavenly to have the house to myself," says Debra. "I spend Friday afternoon and evening cleaning like crazy which sounds absurd, but I never (ever) have the opportunity to enjoy a clean house any other time. Call me crazy but I love walking across a freshly scrubbed floor in my bare feet knowing that no one is going to spill cereal or crackers on it for the next two days. Then I spend time watching my favorite movies, ordering Chinese, taking naps and just having fun doing nothing. It's like having a mini-vacation. By the time my family rolls in Sunday night, I'm just beginning to miss them (and their rambunctious noise). It is a great weekend for everyone, and once my mother-in-law came to grips with the fact that I was not abandoning my family for folly, it has worked out just fine."

See, every woman's idea of time for herself is different and that's OK! The key to rejuvenating is to admit that you deserve to spend some time to yourself and then find ways to give yourself exactly what you need.

CONCLUSION

Well, our discussion about how to survive the chaos of your homeschool and turn it into a calmer environment for the entire clan is over. I hope you noticed the most important theme of the book ... do you know what it is? As promised, it wasn't about which curriculum to choose or even how to teach your children specific subjects. The goal of this book was to help you and every homeschooling mom out there come to grips with the fact that it is all about her. If she fails to take care of herself first, her family will fall apart and her homeschool efforts will fail.

Take a tip from our Lord and Savior, Jesus. He was the ultimate homeschooler, trying to teach the world about salvation one household (or town) at a time. It got to Him too (just like it gets to you). So what did He do? When He needed to be alone and spend time in serious prayer, He left the crowds and his disciples and did what he knew He should: he took some time to rejuvenate and regroup. If Jesus, the busiest man of all time (with such a short time to do such a big job) could take a day or two to replenish his physical, emotional and spiritual self, why do mothers have such a difficult time admitting that we need an hour a day for ourselves?

It takes a strong leader to run a school, and Mom, you can't be that strong administrator without forging past the motherlode of guilt you have put upon yourself and actually take care of the most important person in your home: YOU!

If you walk away with anything from these pages, I hope it is that you are just as important as everyone else in your home and yes, the little things do matter. Taking just 15 minutes in the morning to indulge in a cup of coffee is not just OK, it's necessary. Scaling back your children's activities to leave you some time each week to get together with friends or do something just for you will only help you better prepare for the week ahead. The only way to stay balanced within is to take the time necessary to nourish yourself.

Your children deserve the best and that includes the best you that you can offer. That tired, cranky you just aren't the mom or the teacher they want or deserve, so simplify your home and school life and get back to being the person you know you can and want to be. Ditch the supermom mentality and opt for the best mom you can be instead.

A few months ago someone asked what I would want placed on my tombstone when I die. I knew right away what the best inscription could be:

"She did her best and it was good enough."

That's how I want my kids to remember me: as a woman who did her best to take care of her family and succeeded in her efforts. That doesn't mean doing everything or being perfect. It just means being good enough. Now that is something to strive for. I used to think that being good enough was somehow a failure, Then, one morning while reading Genesis, it dawned on me. In each verse, after

God made a new part of the world, he looked at his creation and said, "It was good." Not "It was great." Not, "It was fantastic." Not, "It was perfect." The Bible says simply, "It was good." Now, if **good** is good enough for God, the creator of all things, why shouldn't being good be satisfactory to us?

I wish you patience and perseverance, dear reader, as you continue on your homeschool journey. May your days be filled with excitement, fun and lots of learning. Leave the dishes dirty, the floor sprinkled in Cheerios and the old newspapers piled in the corner. Go outside and run in the sprinkler, take a walk with your kids and enjoy the journey ahead – it's the adventure of a lifetime so savor it to the end. There will be plenty of time for clean bathrooms and volunteering in the community. Now is your time to shine at home. So go ahead and say no to everyone who calls with an urgent plea. Liberate yourself and focus on those things you deem most important. Do your very best at the task at hand and you will find your efforts to be not just good enough, but let it be said that "It was good!"